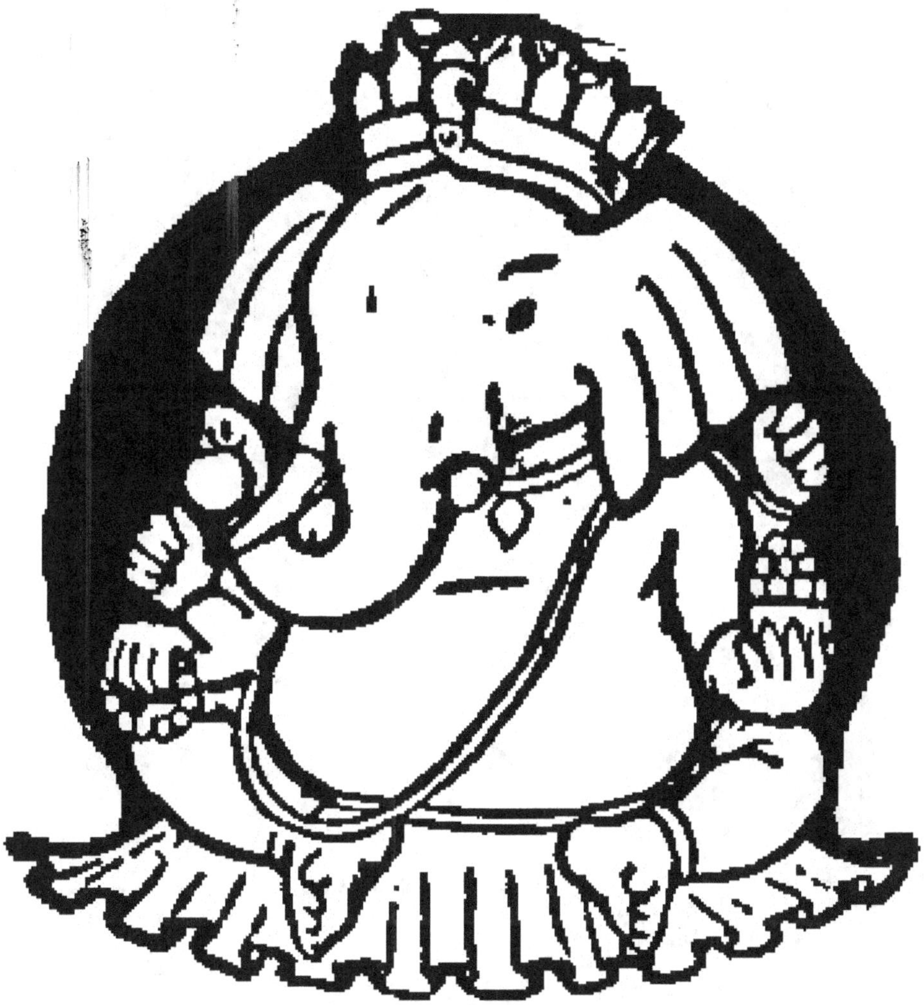

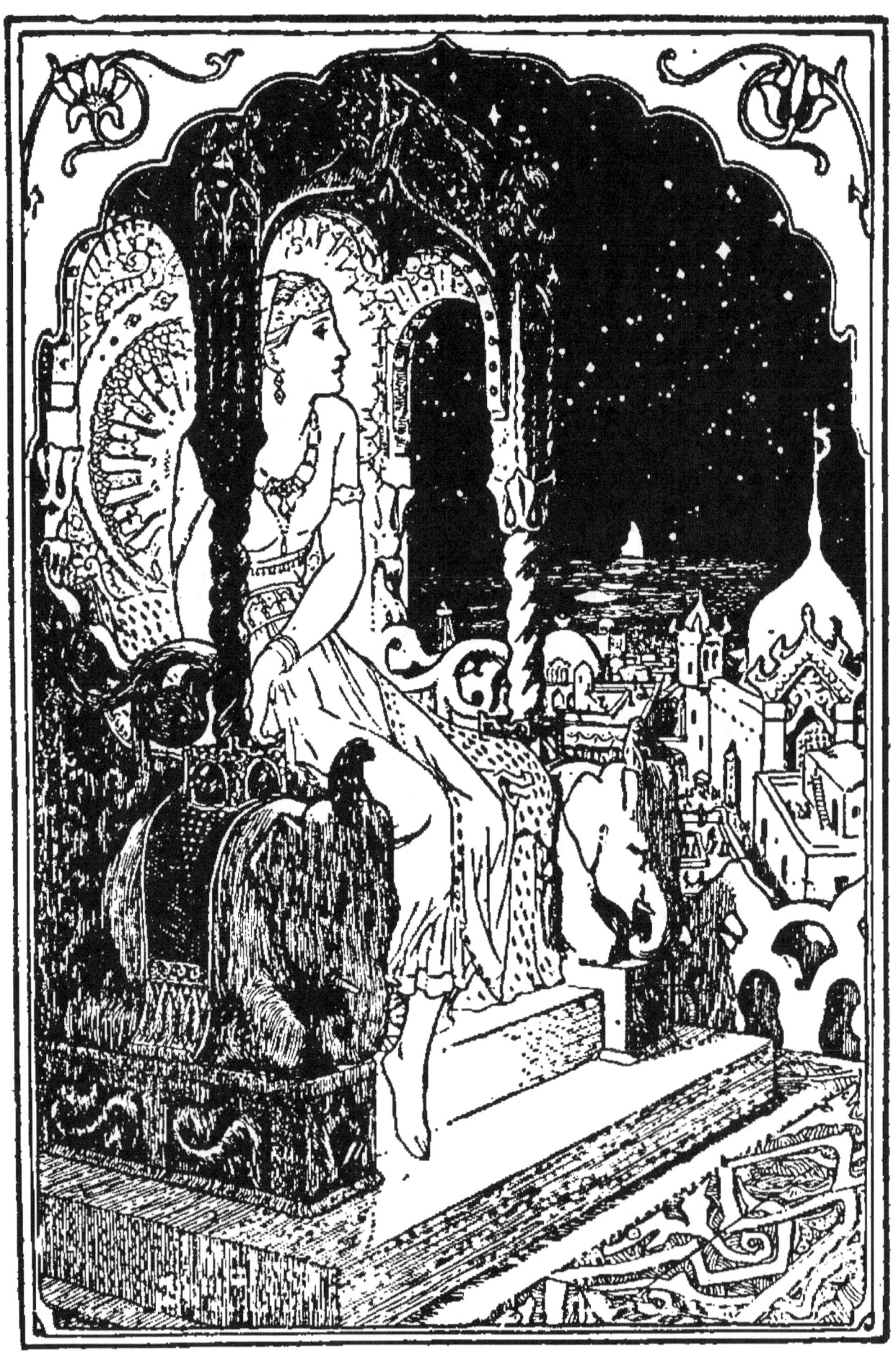

Princess Labam

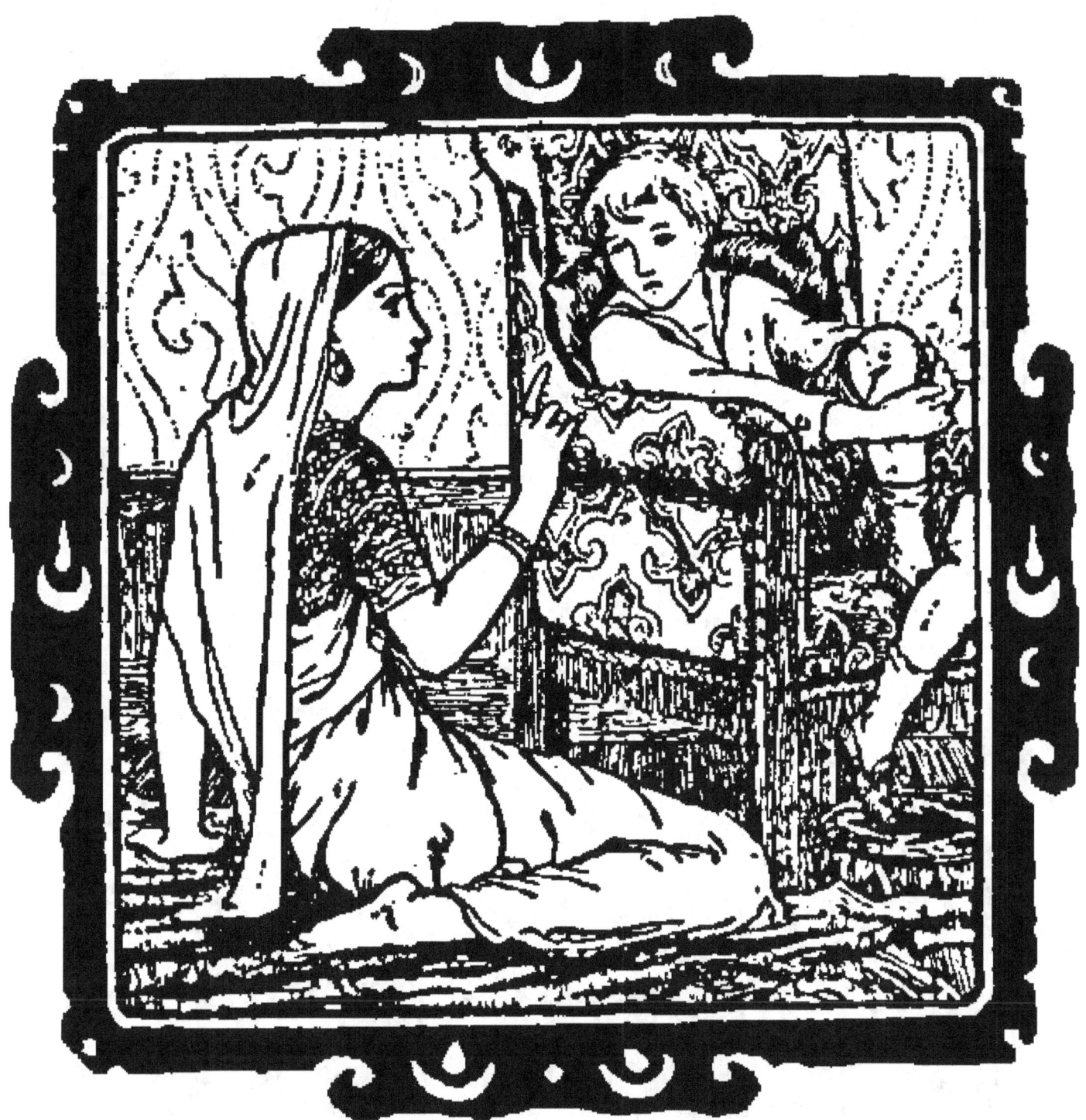

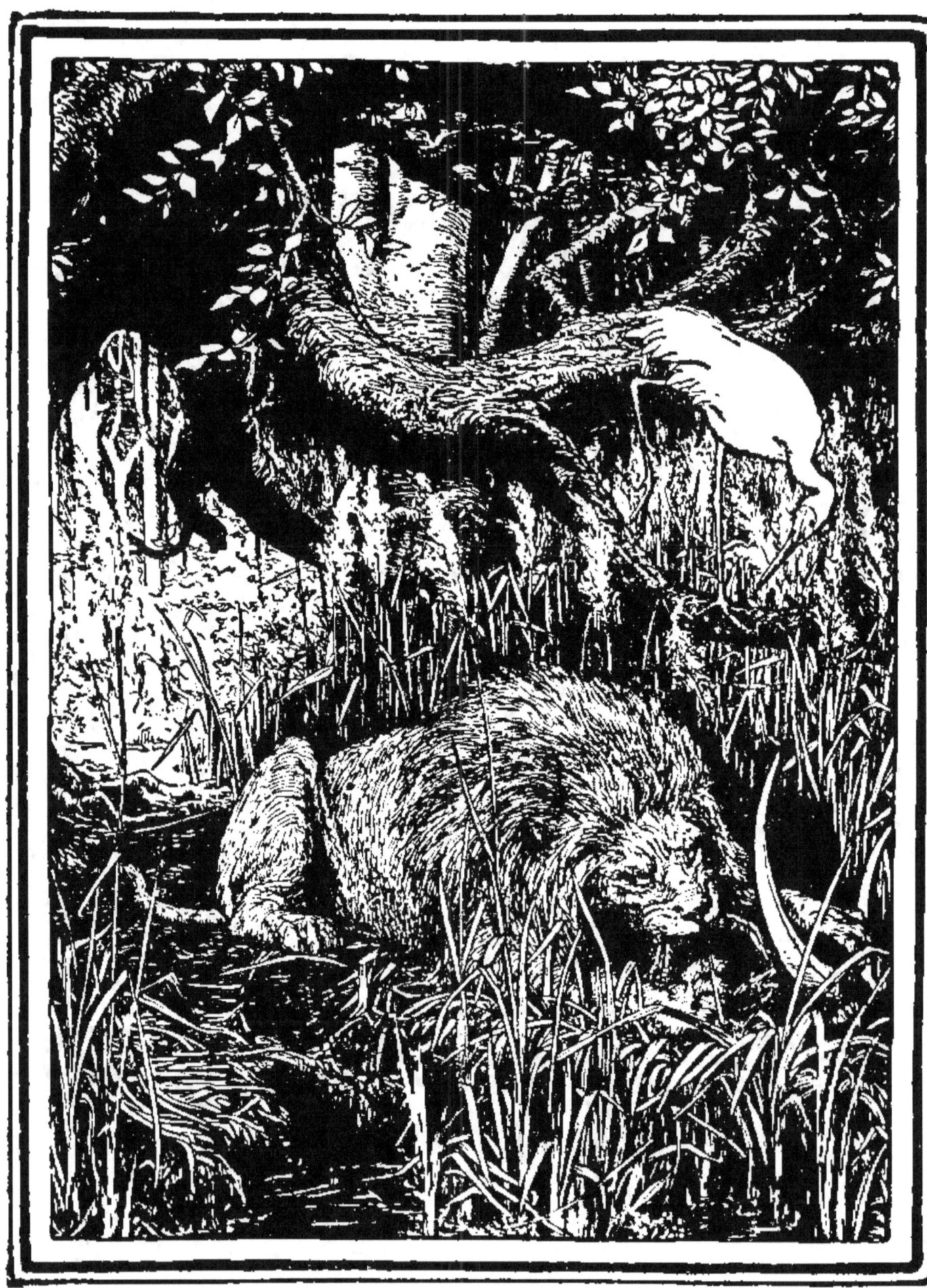

The Lion and the Crane

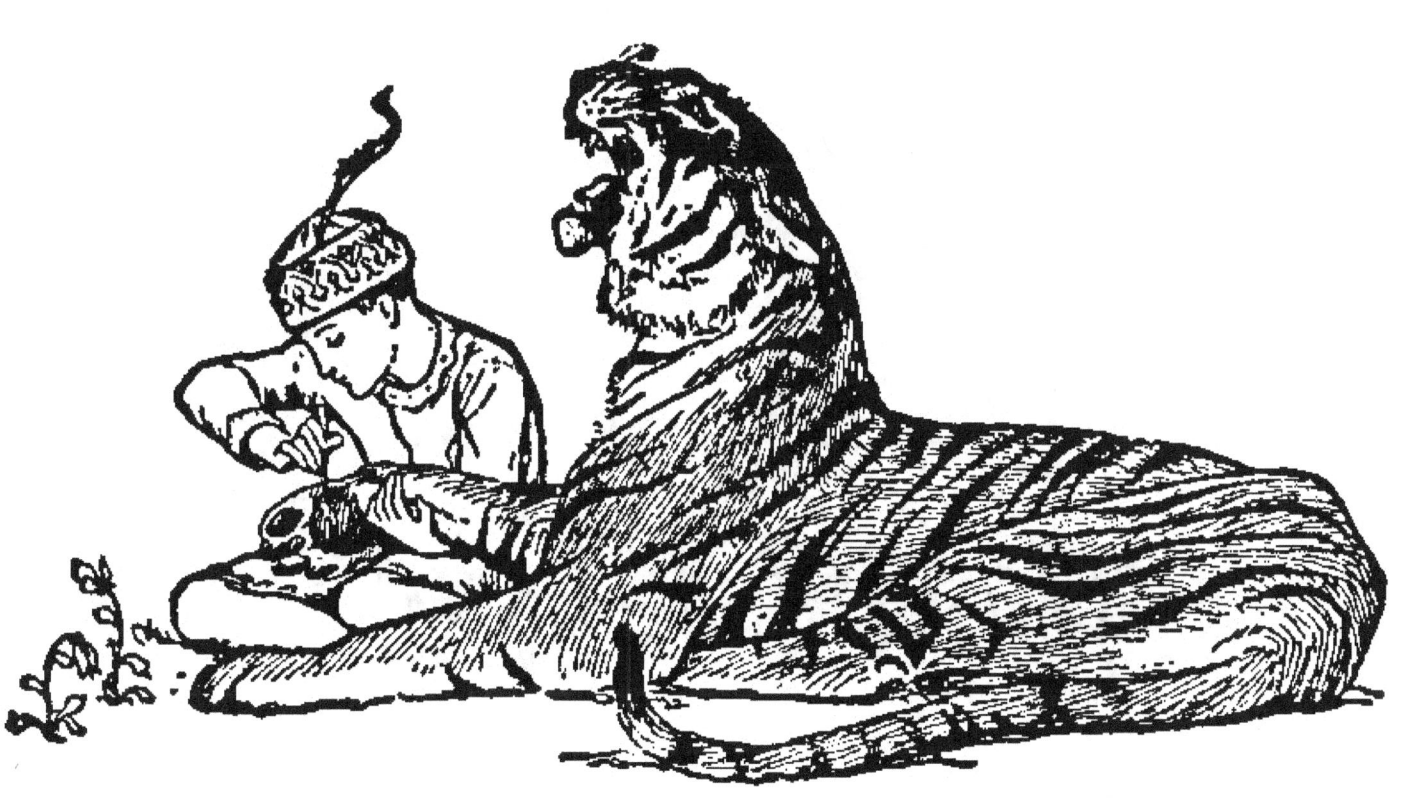

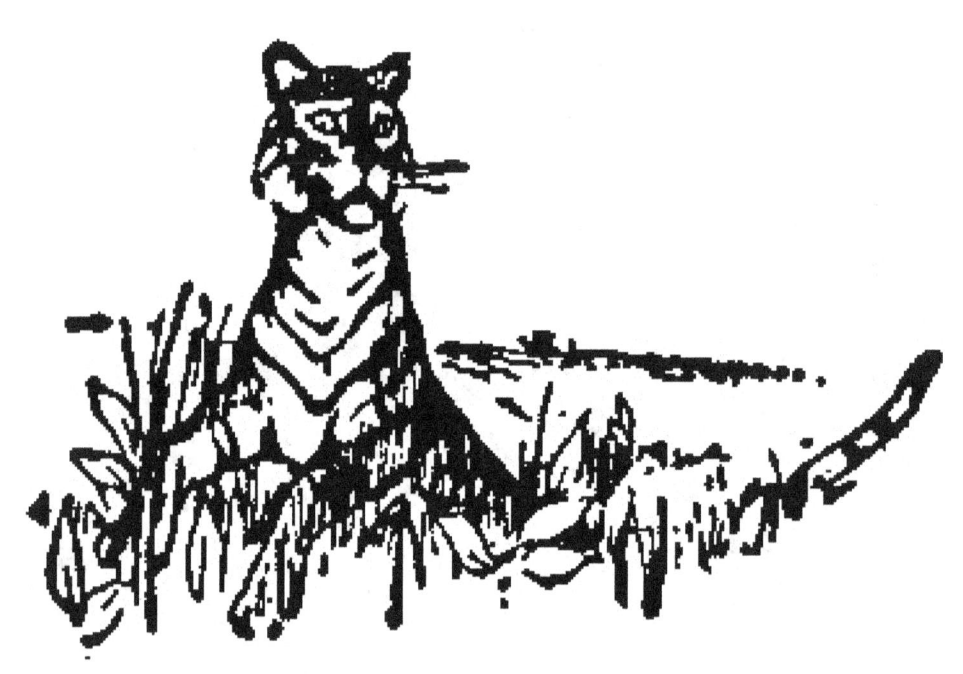

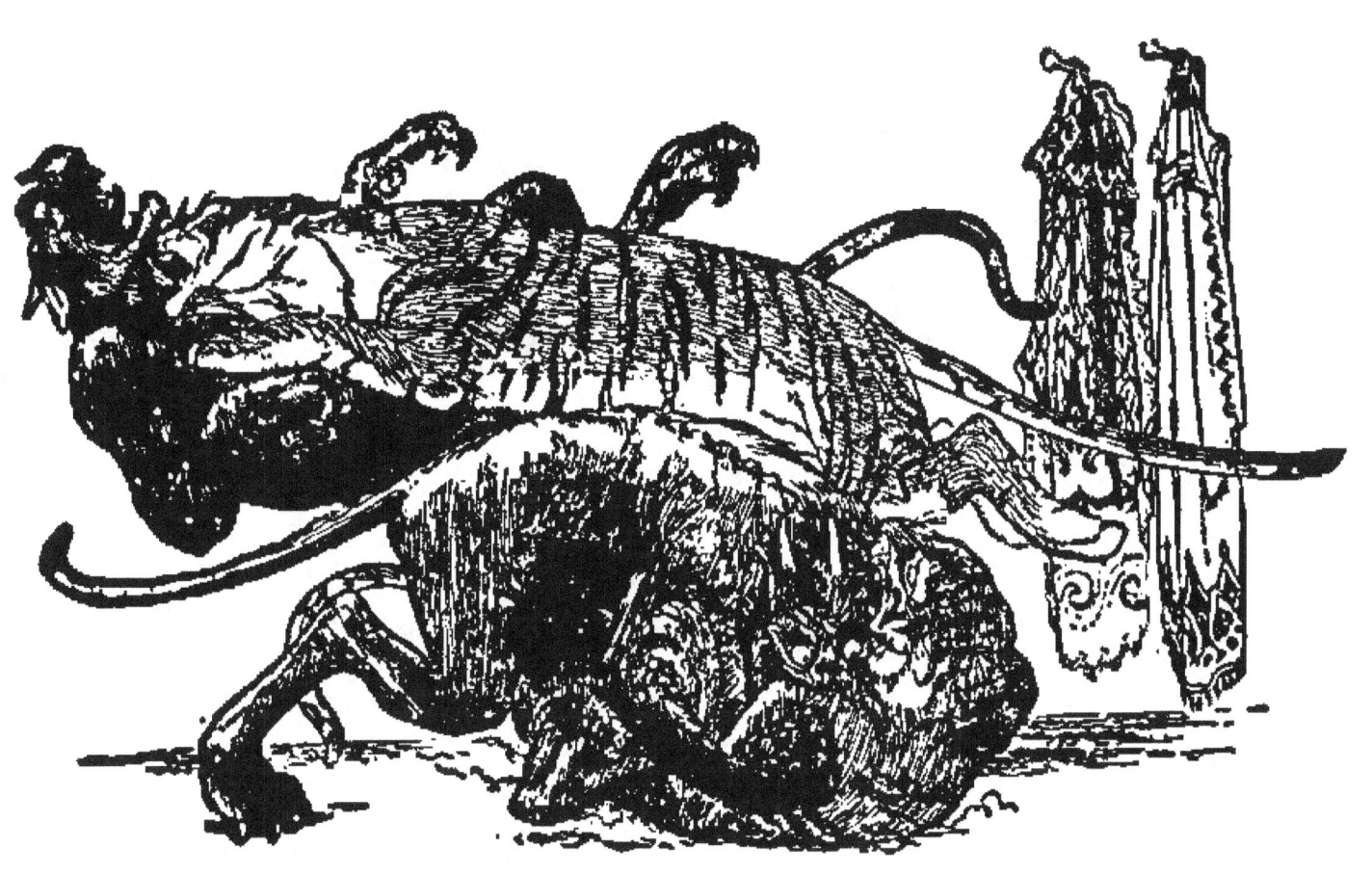

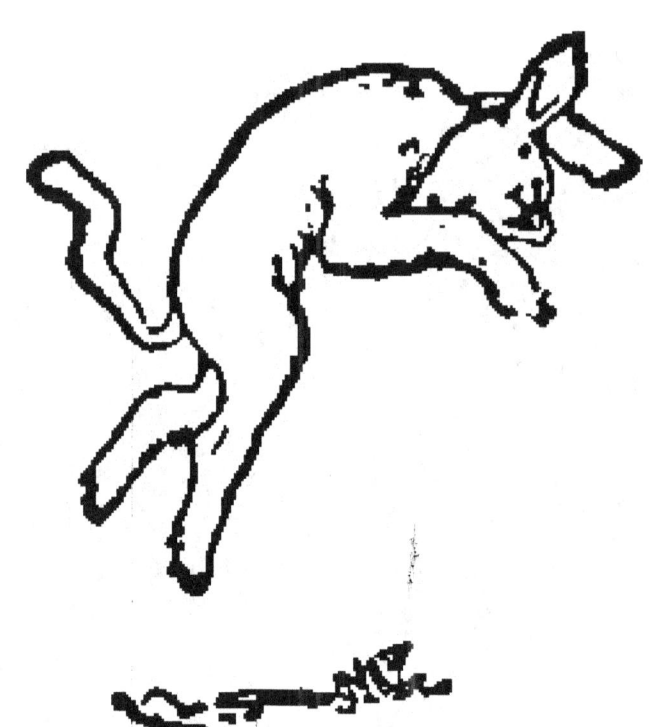

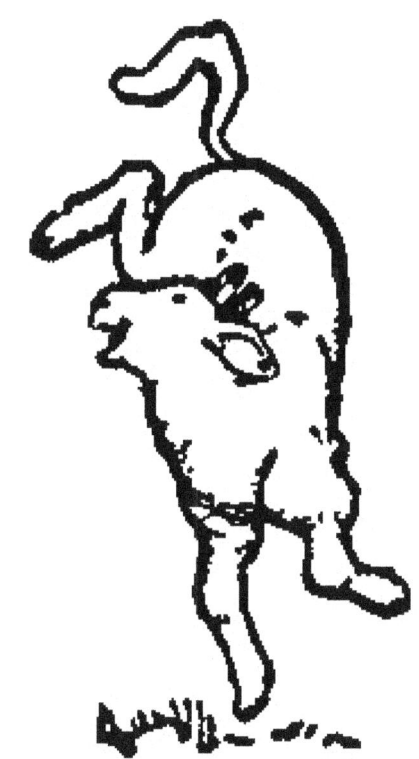

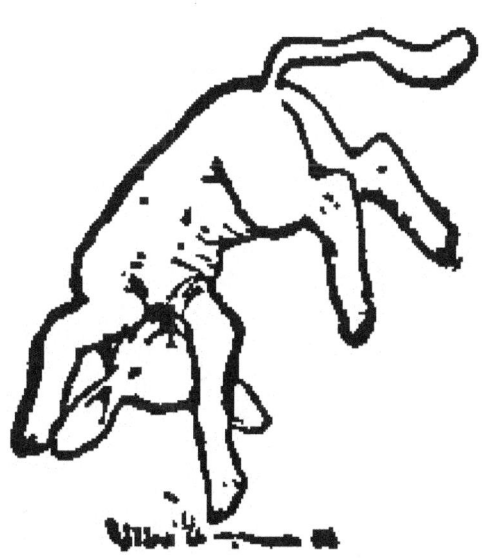

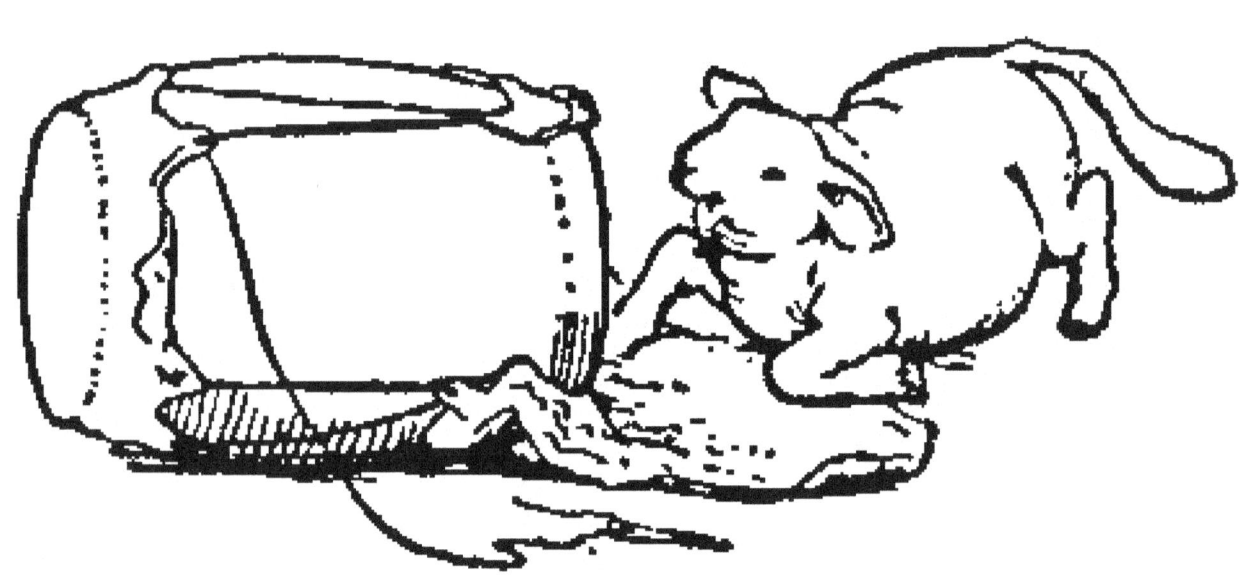

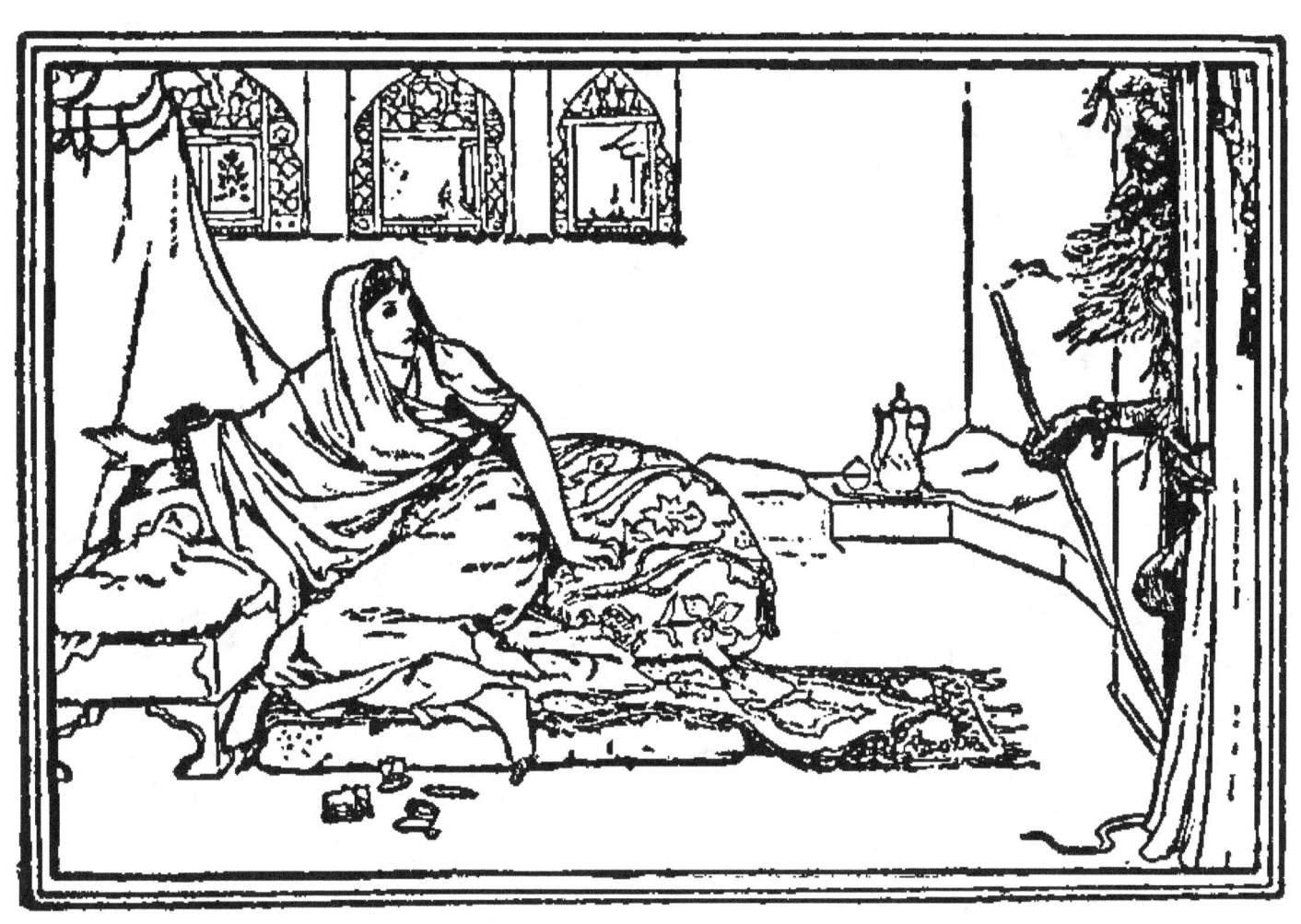

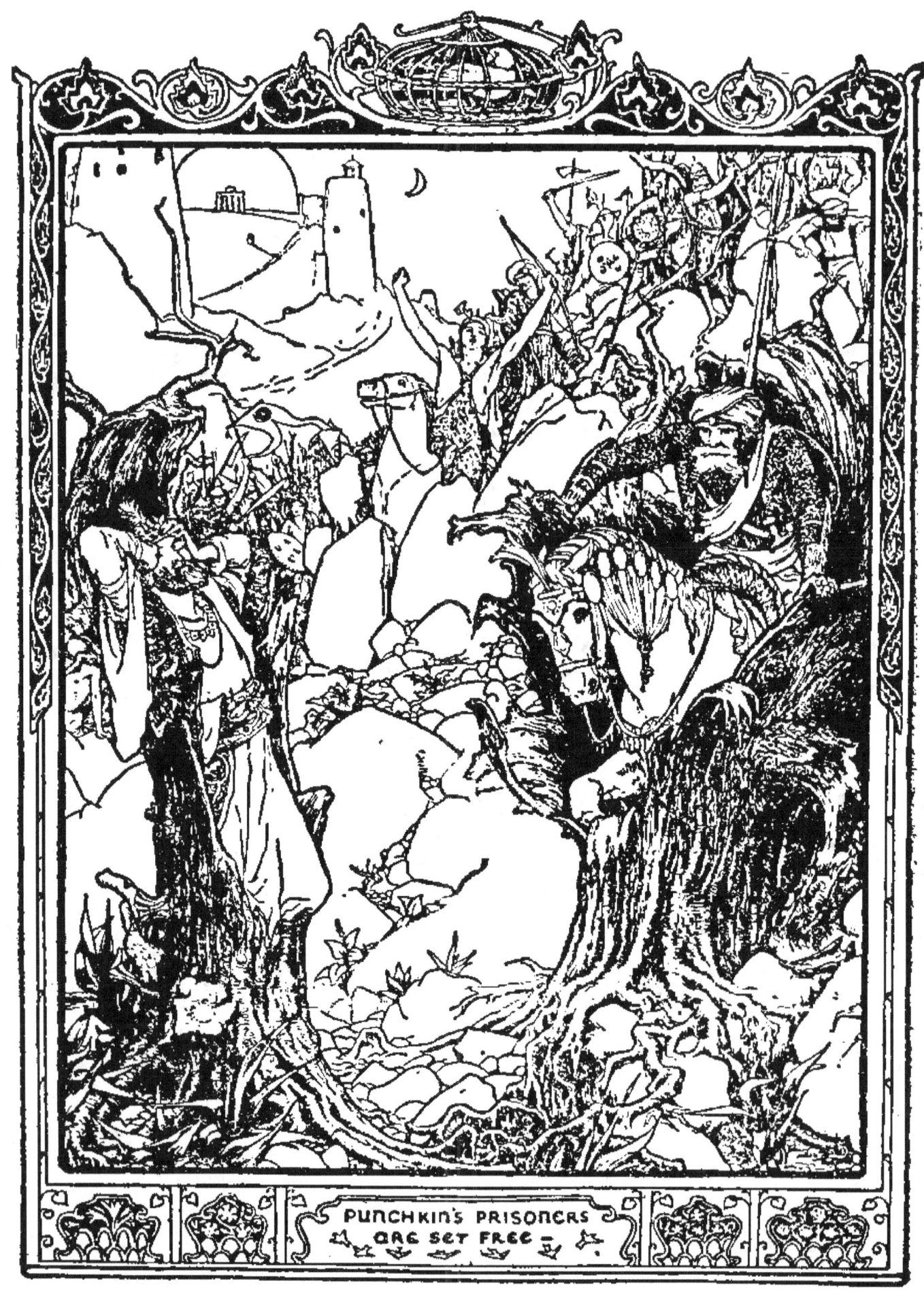

Punchkin's Prisoners are Set Free

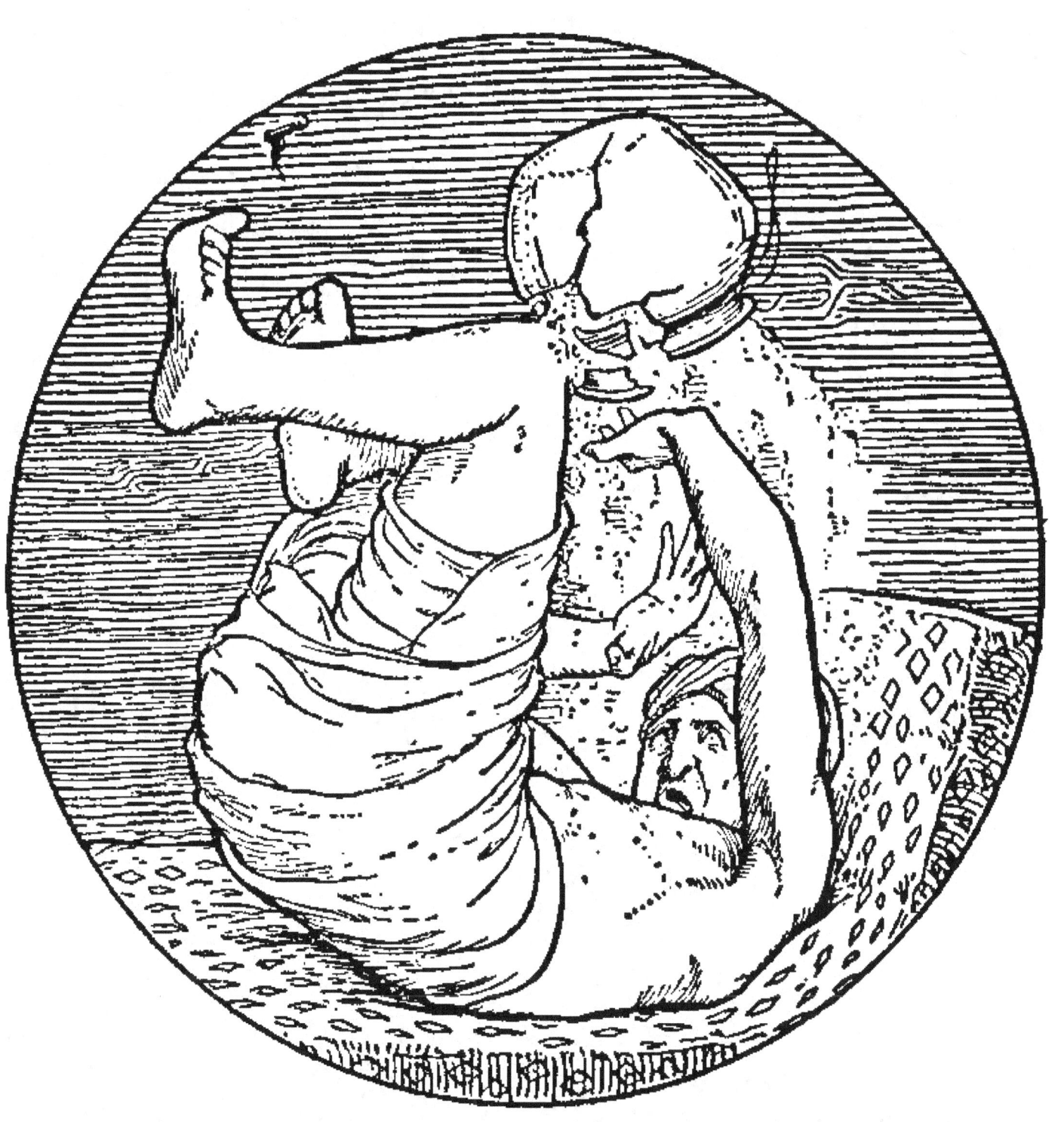

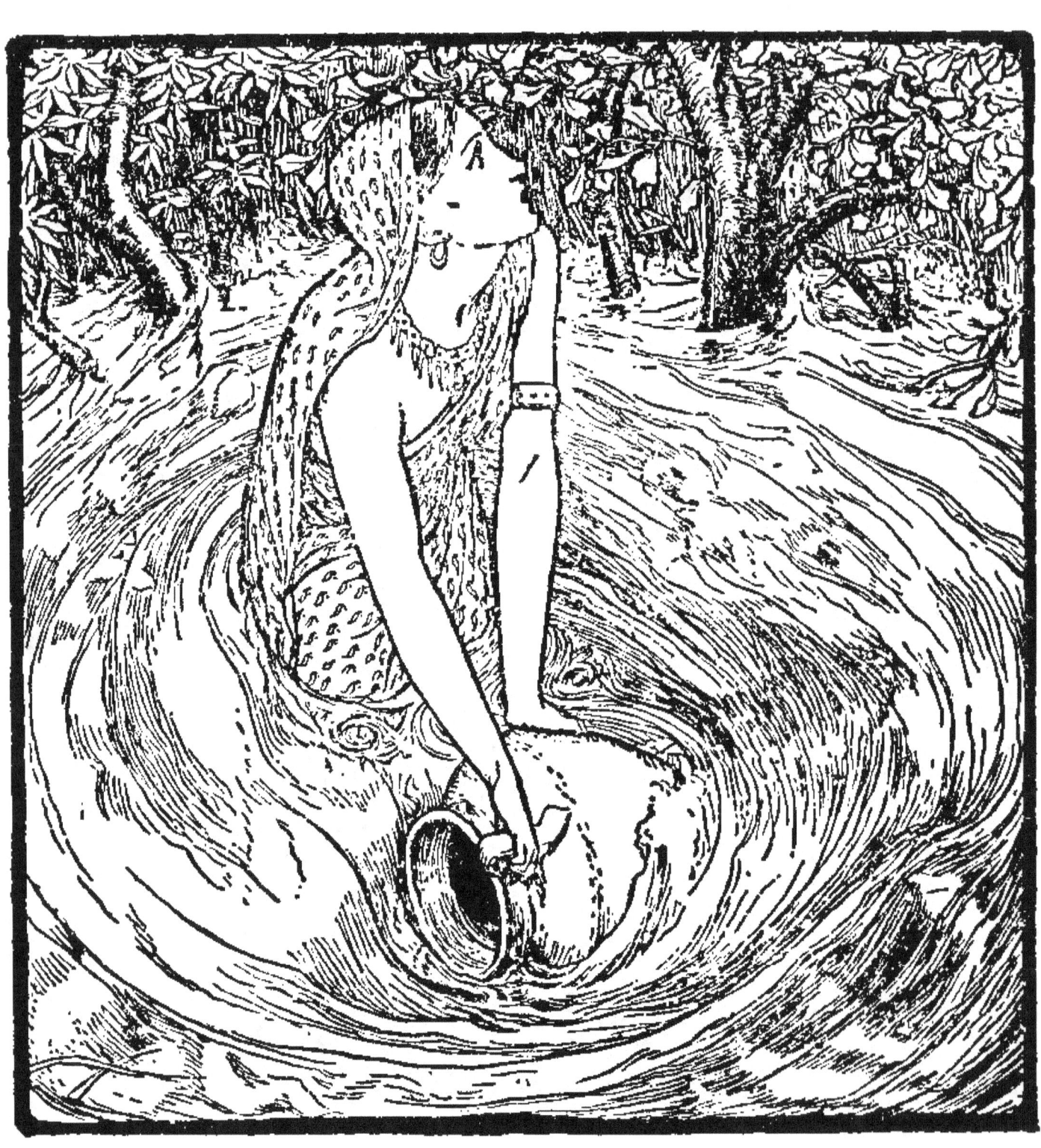

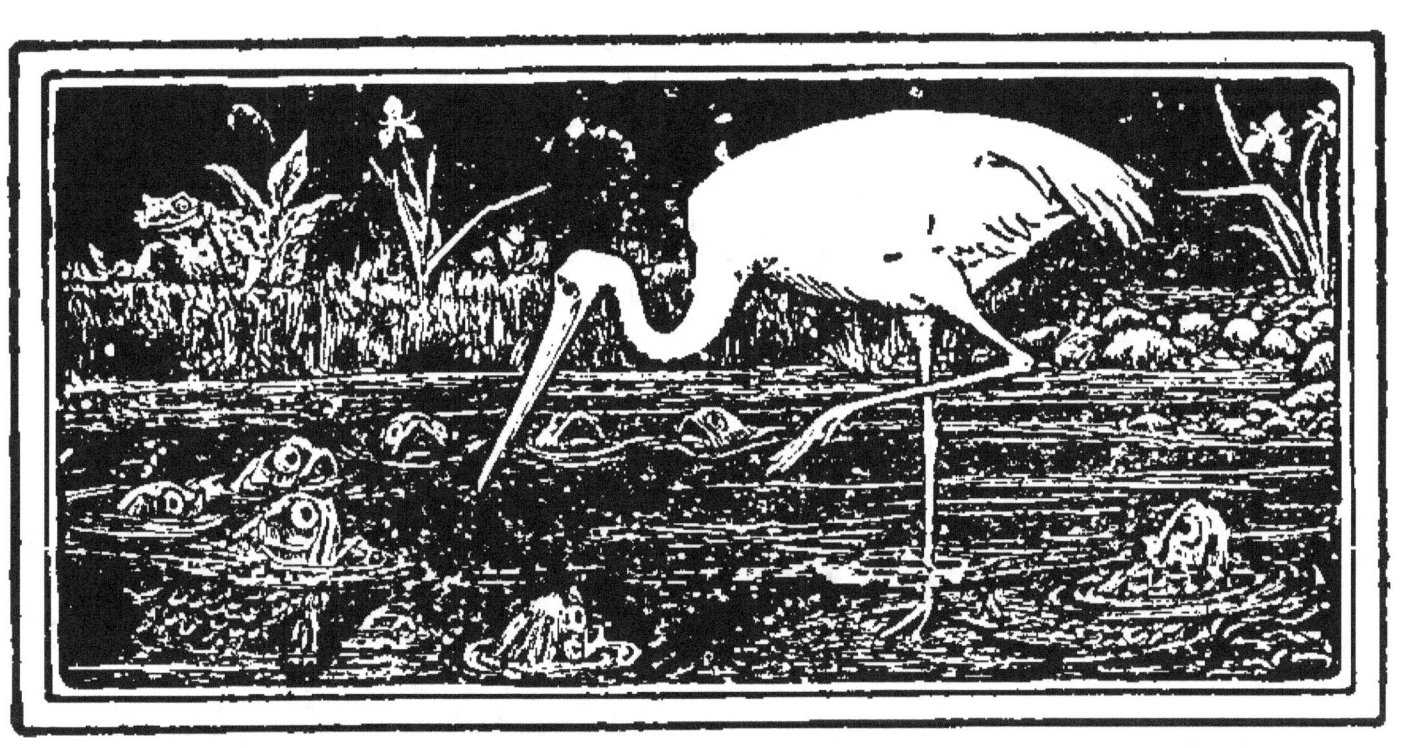

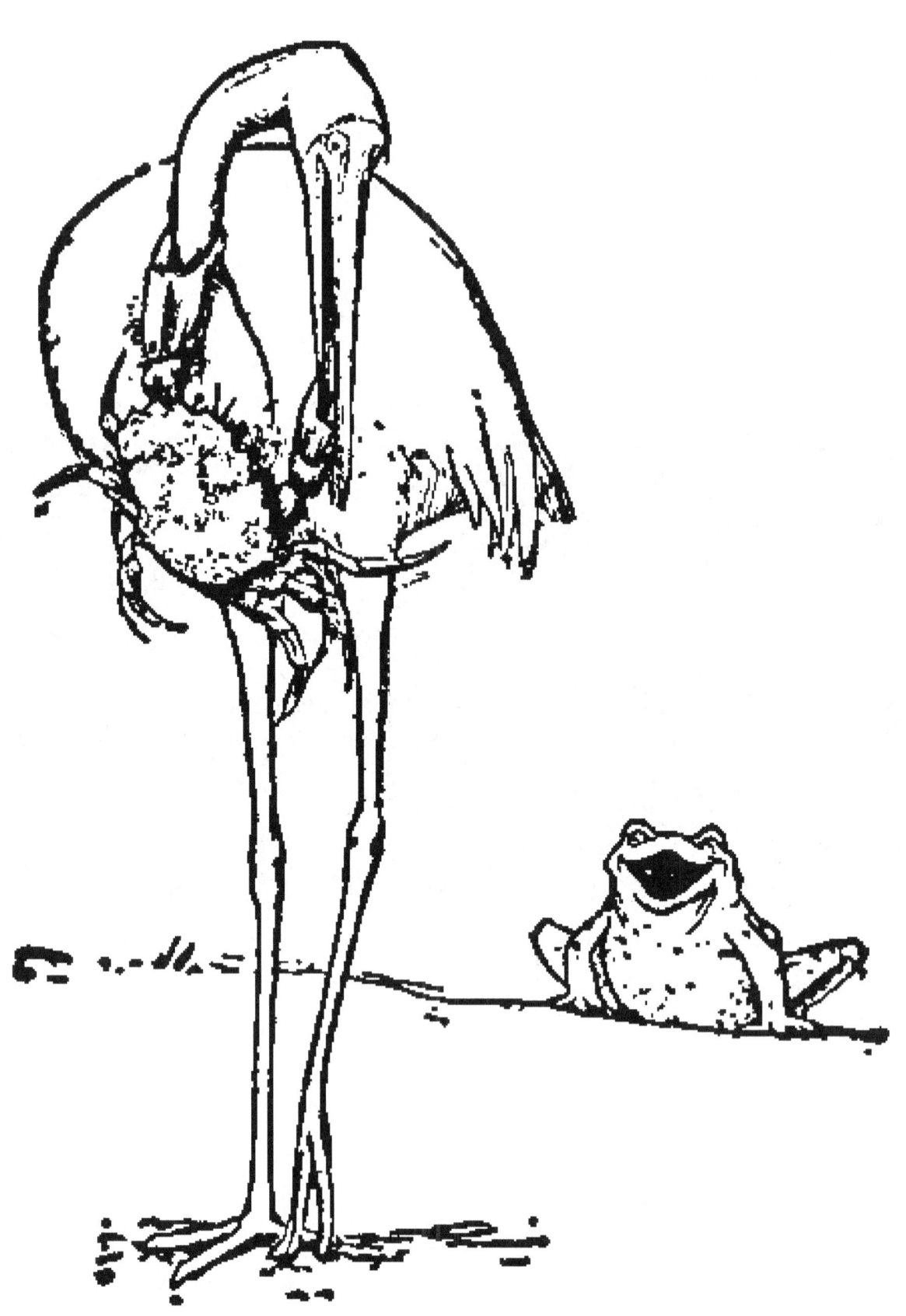

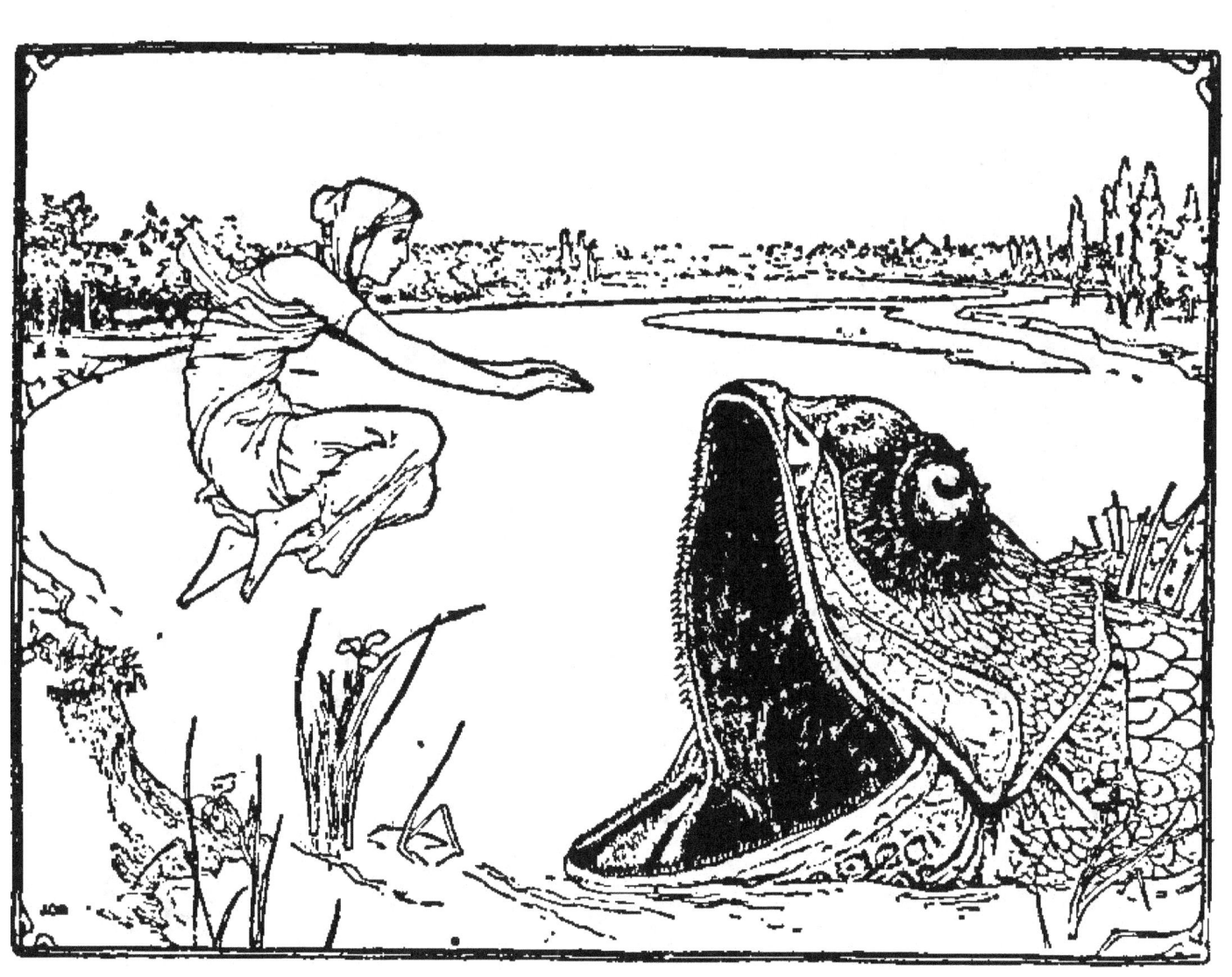

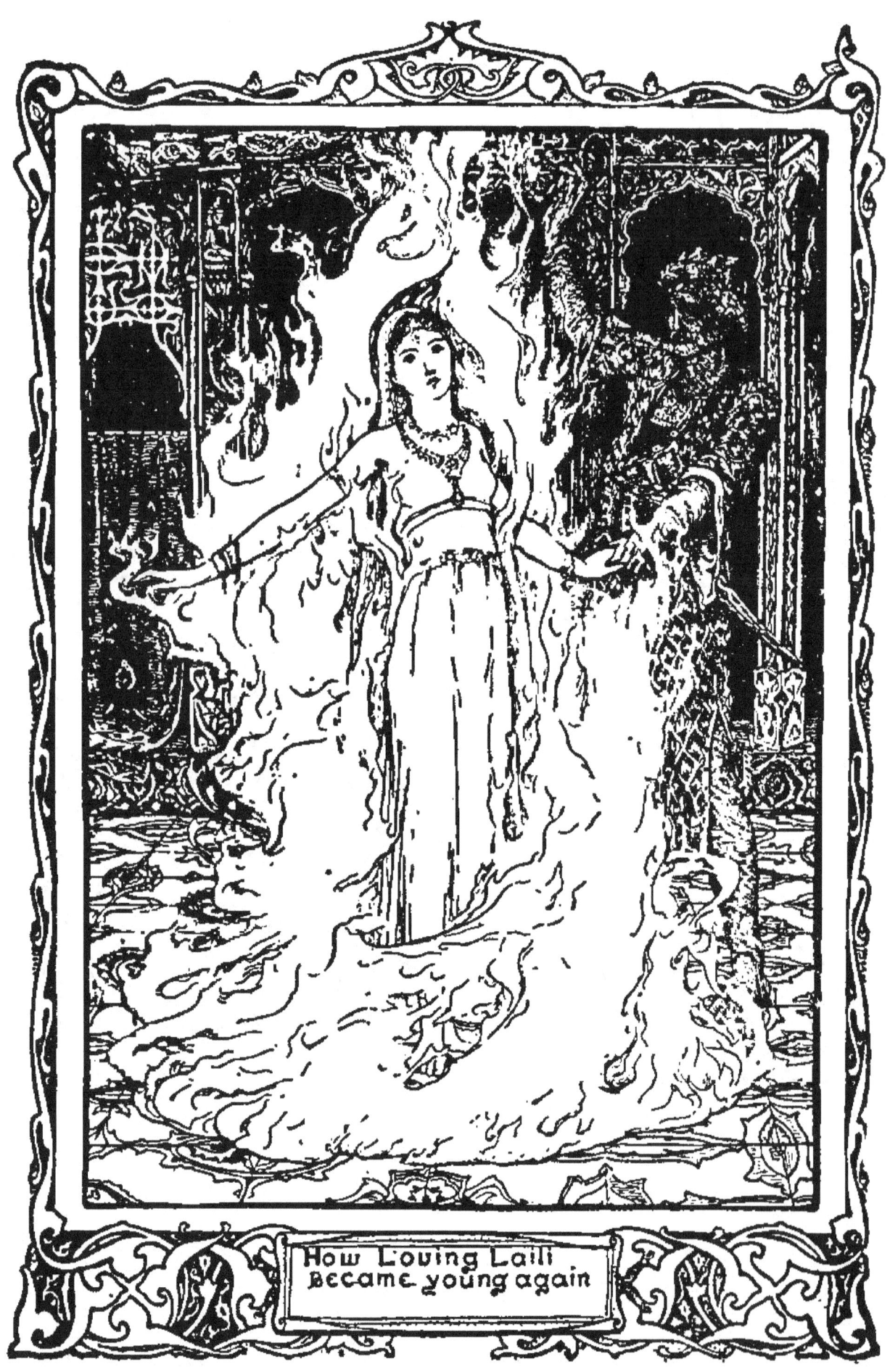

How Loving Laili Became Young Again

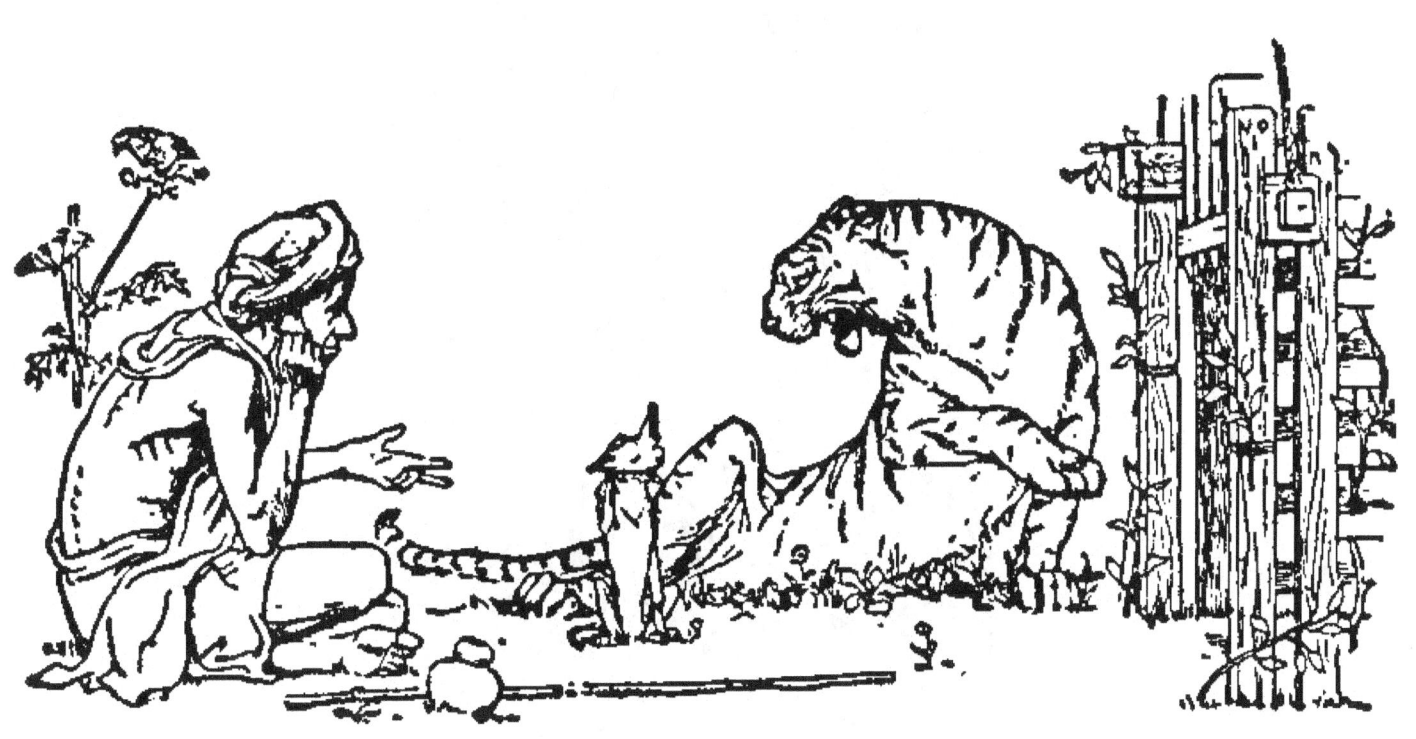

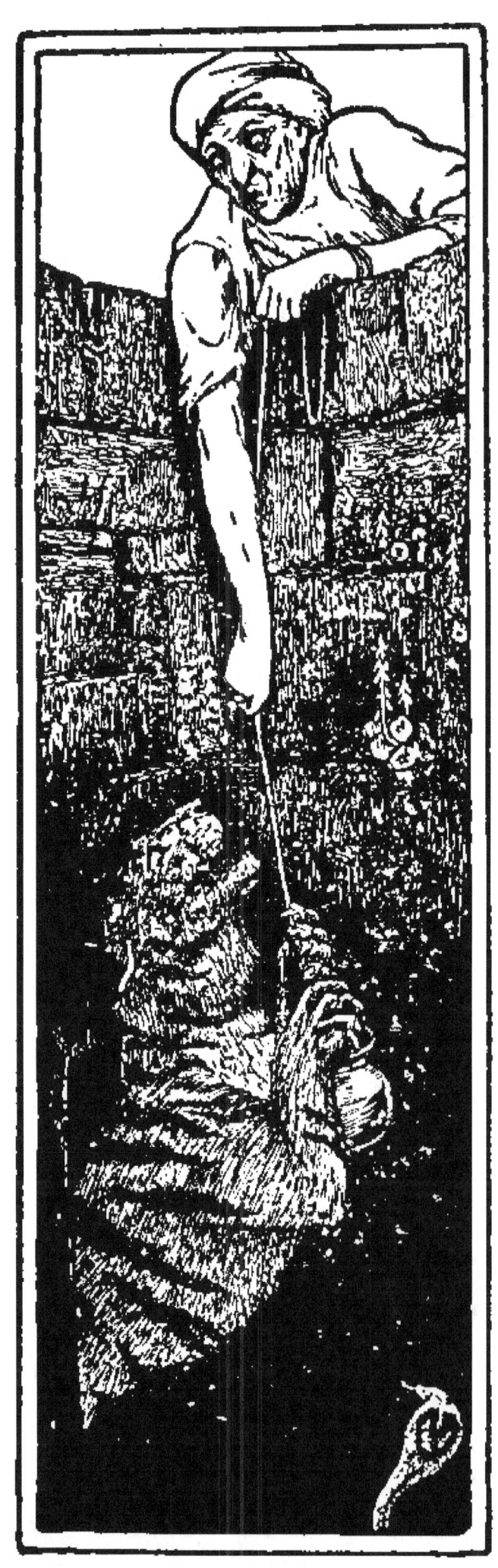

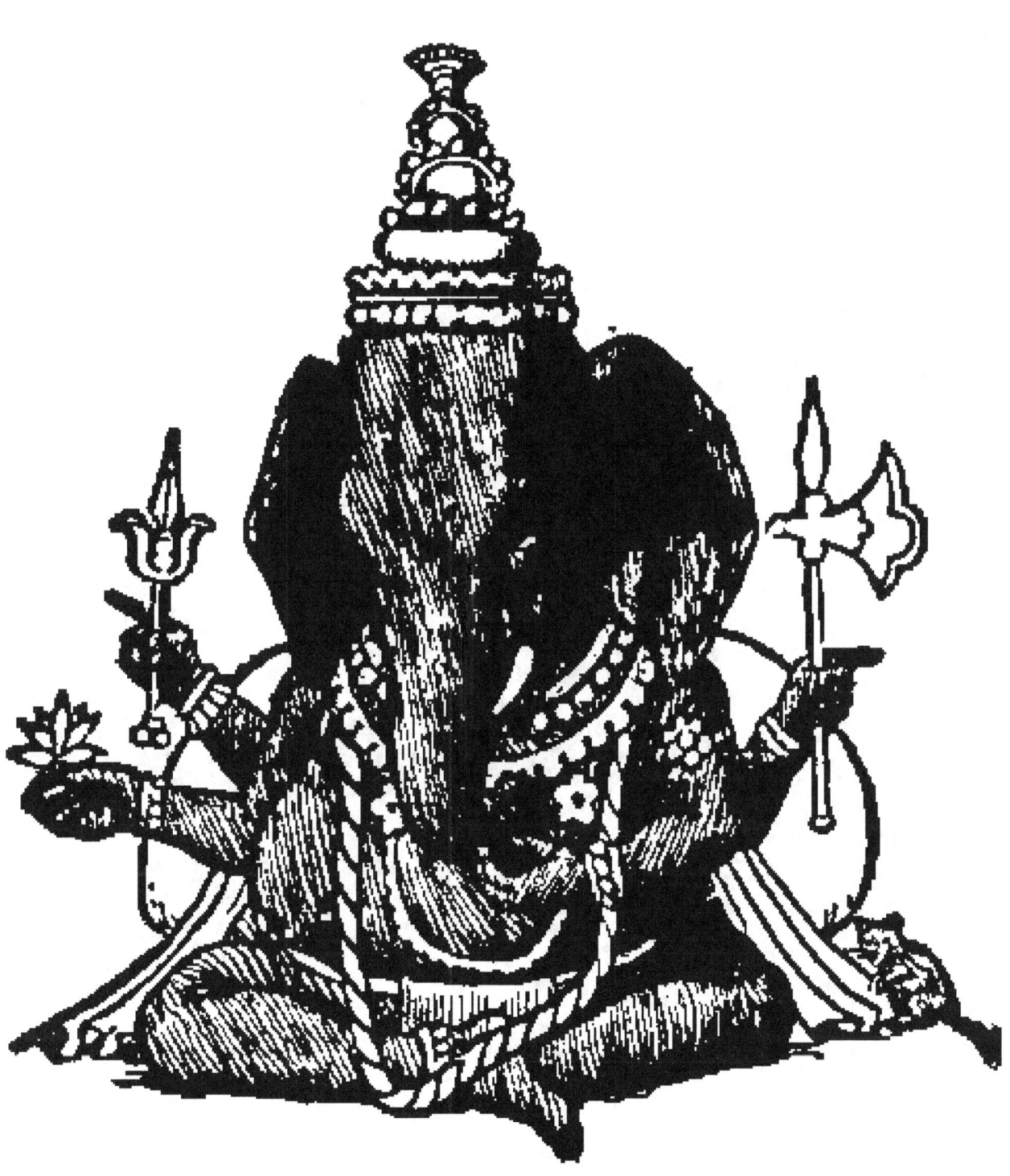

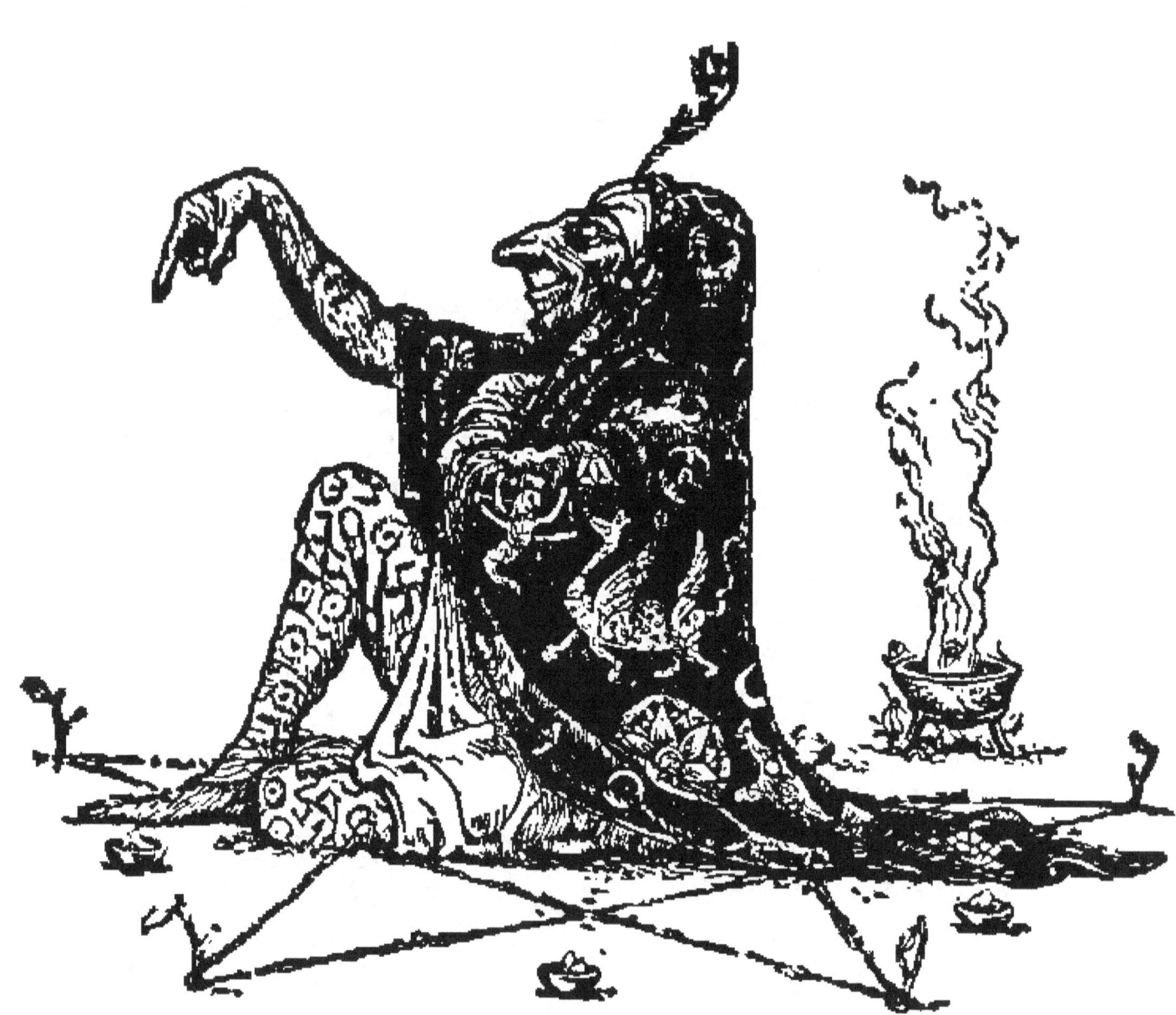

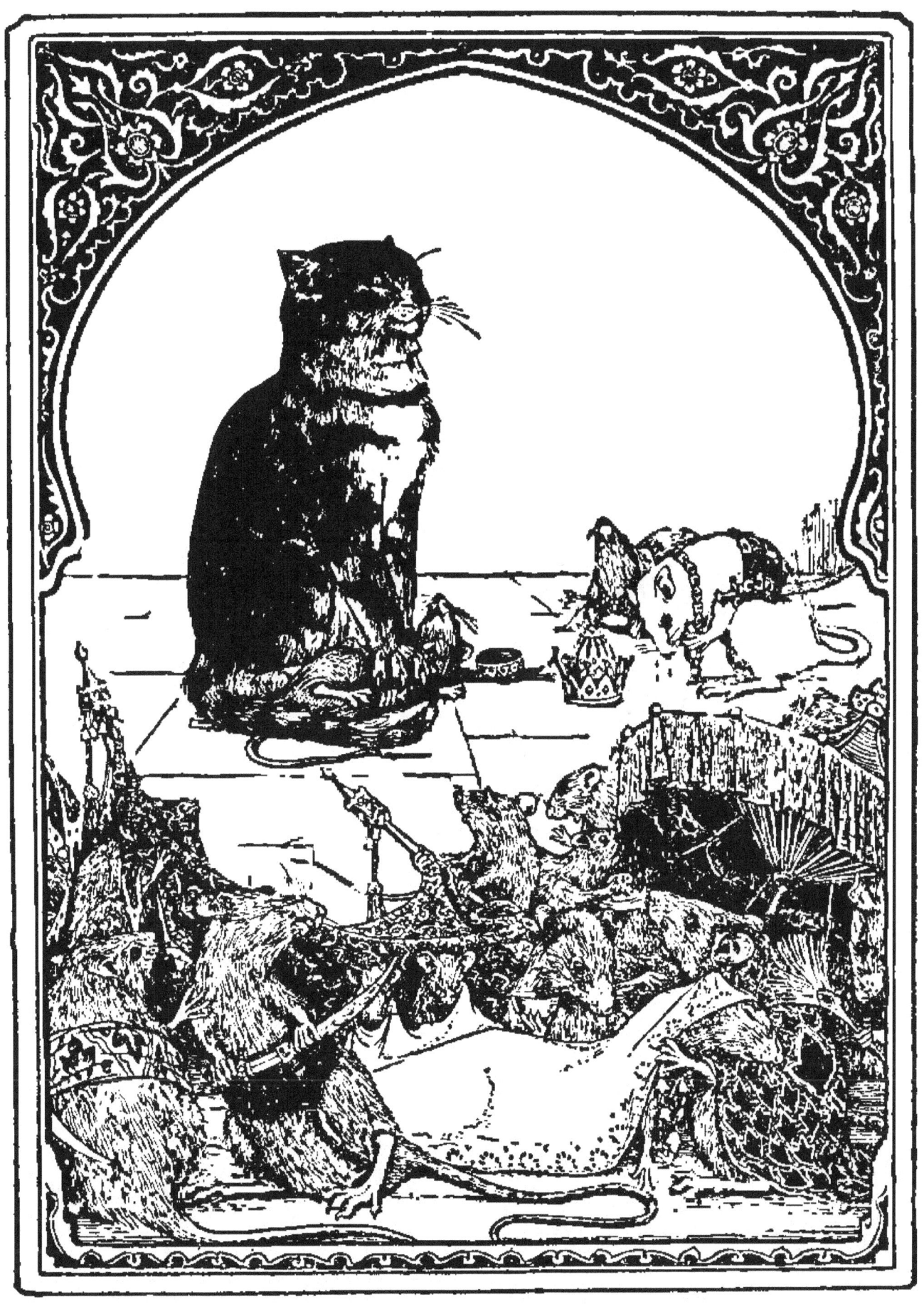

The Charmed Ring

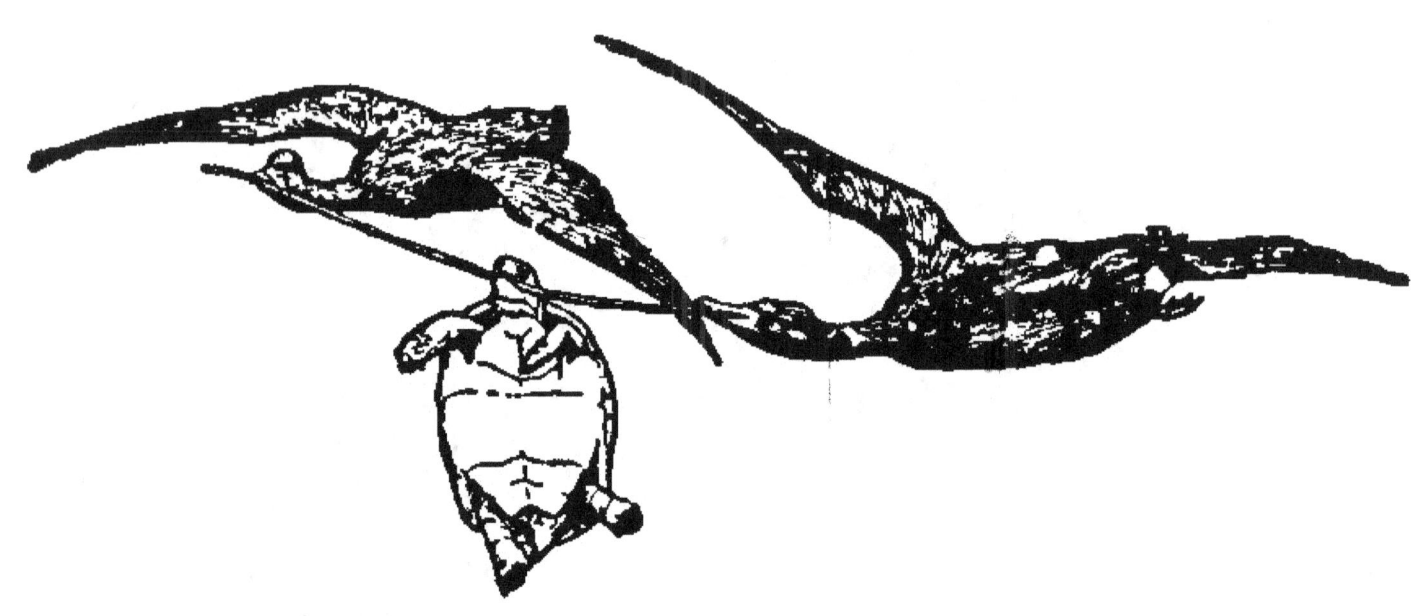

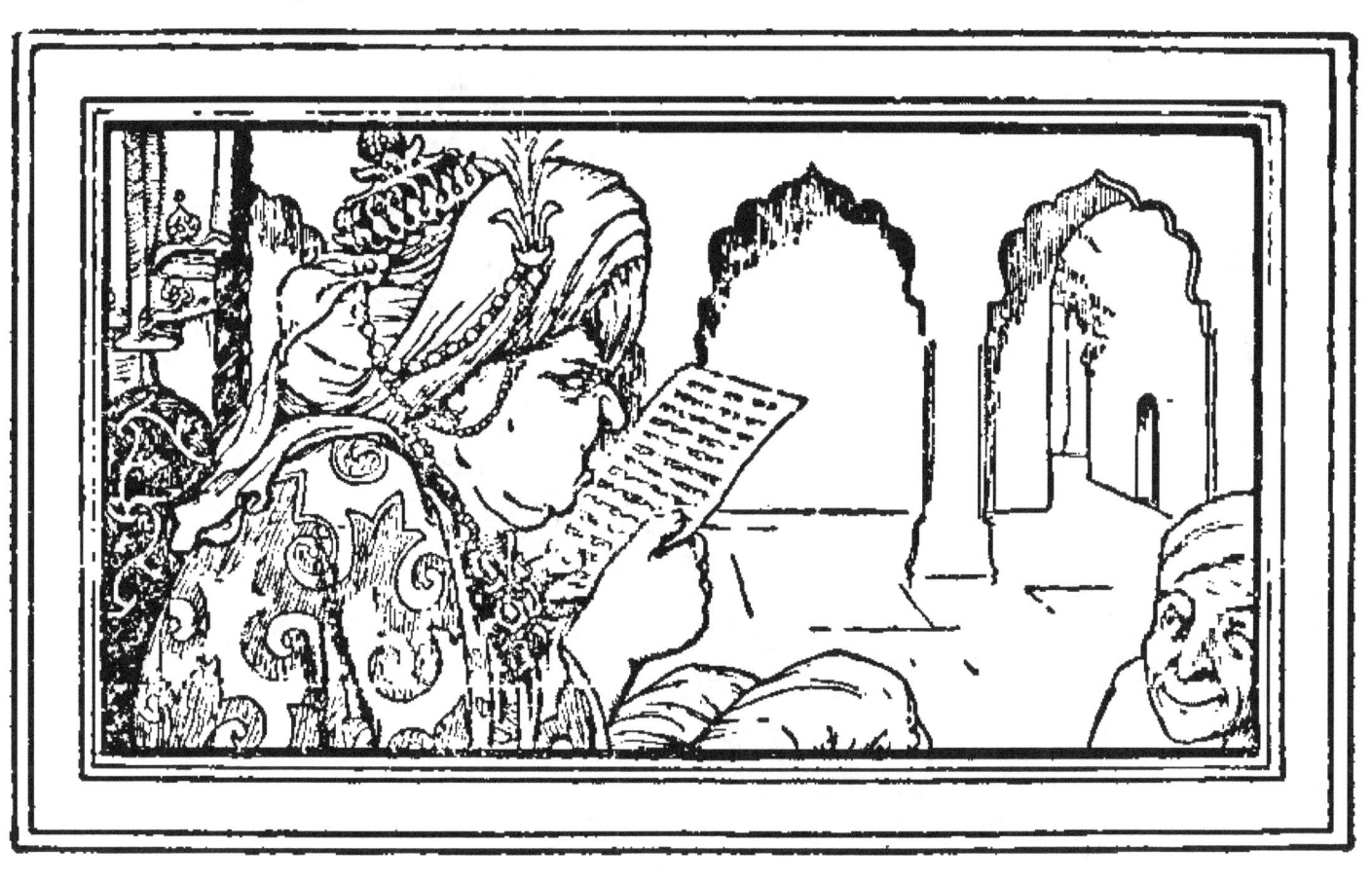

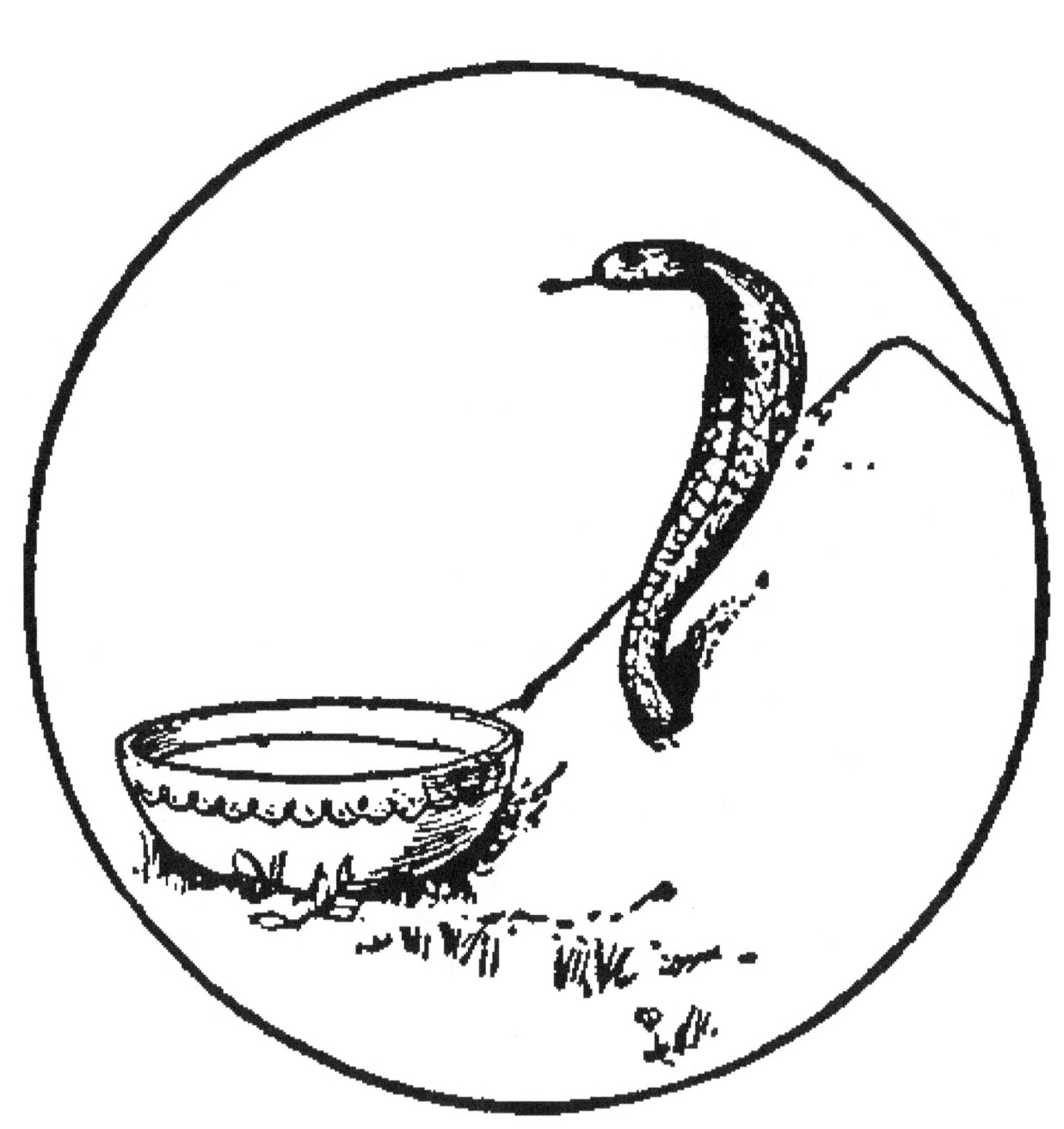

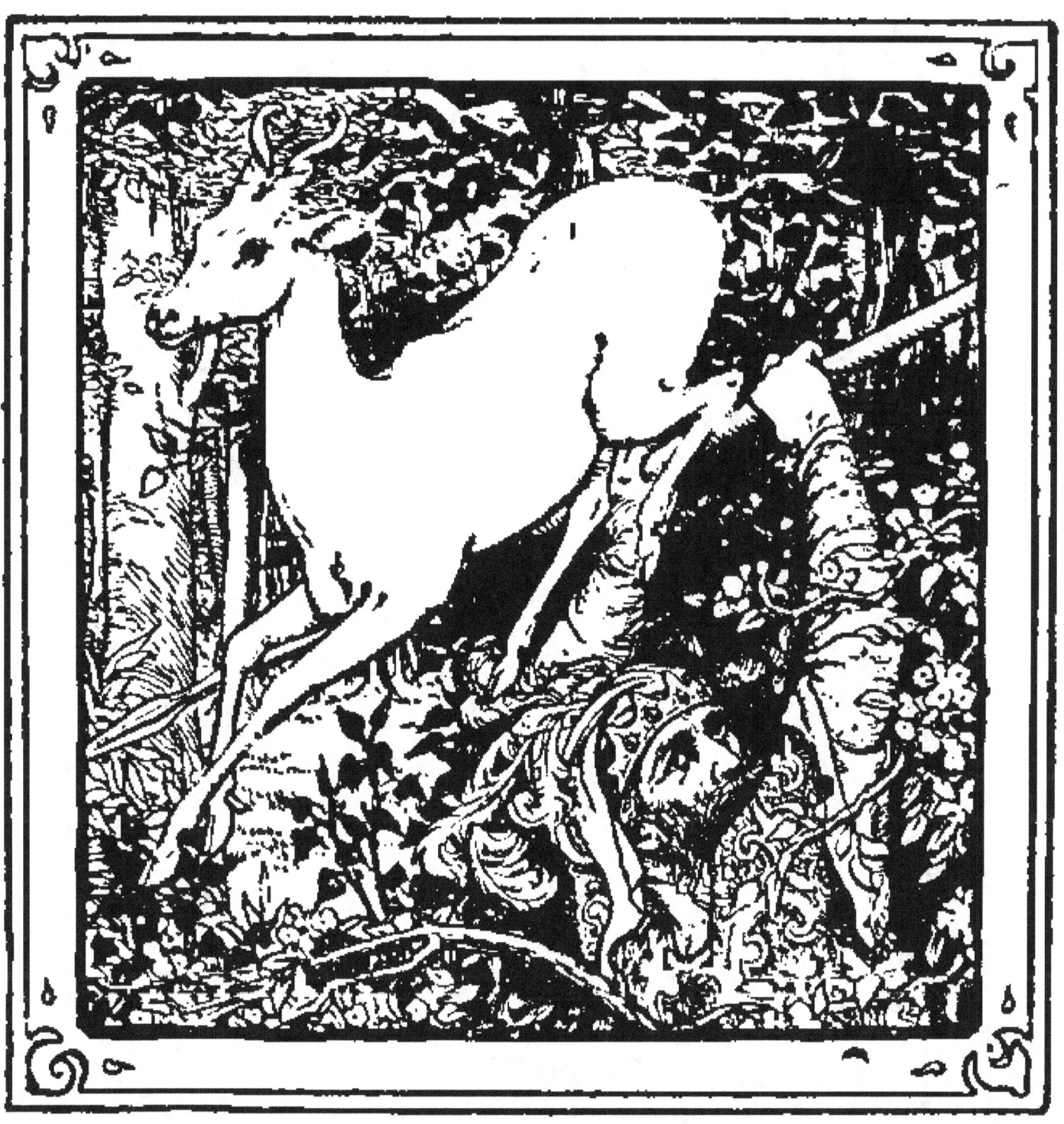

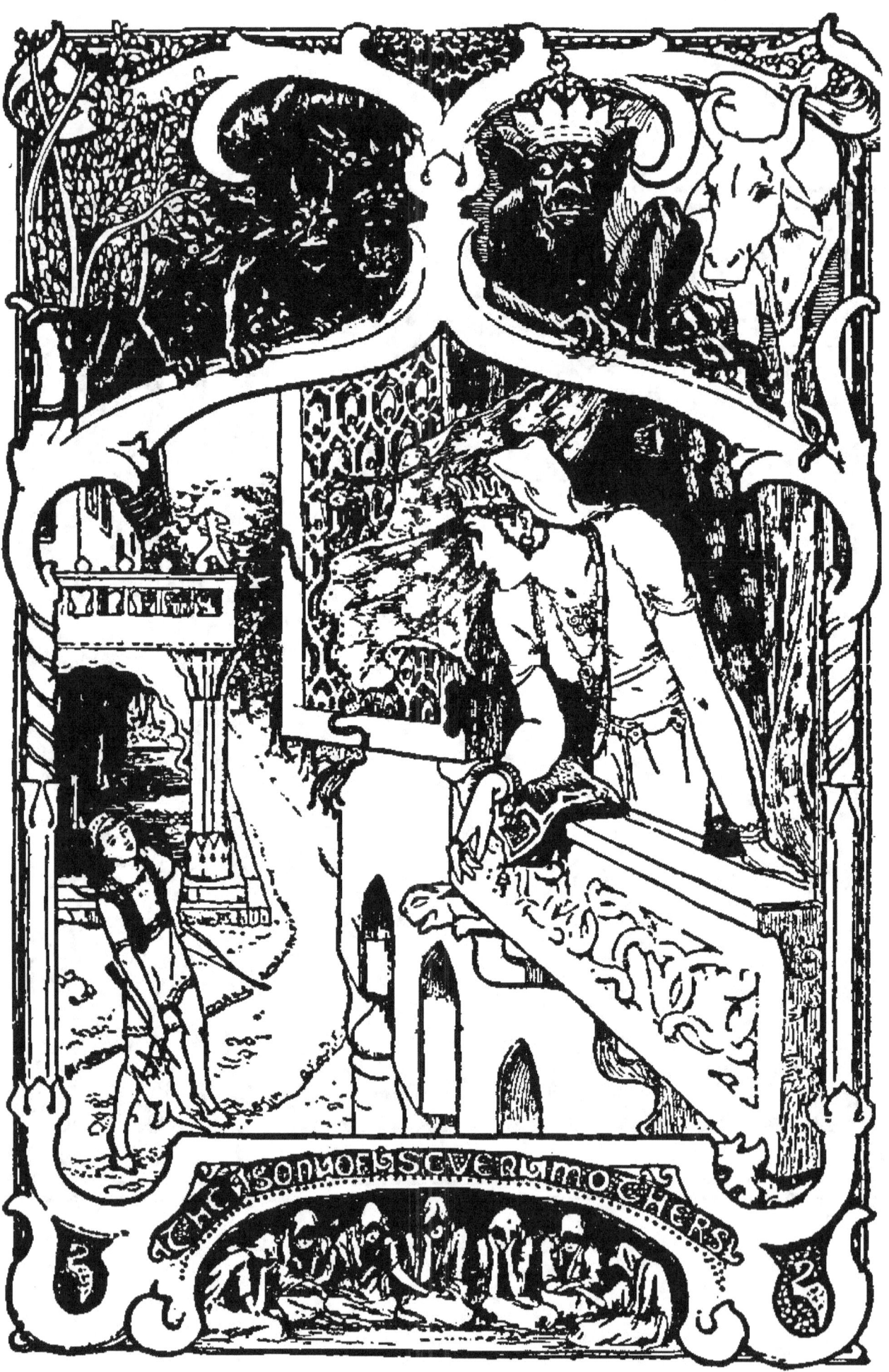
The Son of Seven Mothers

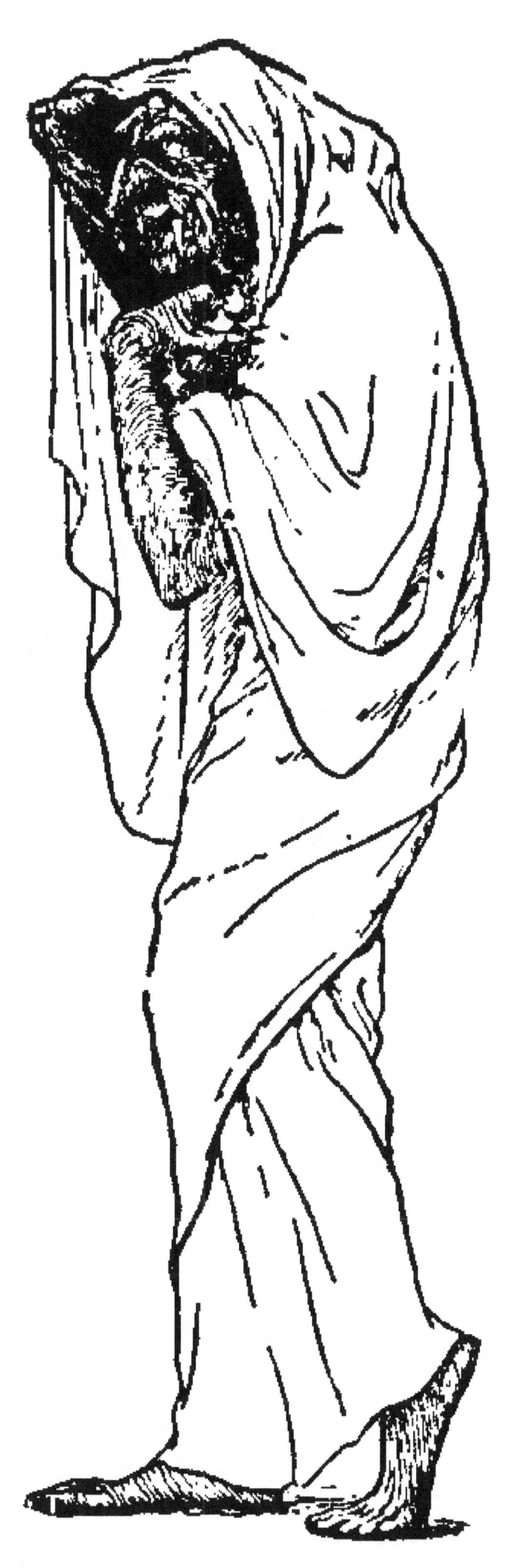

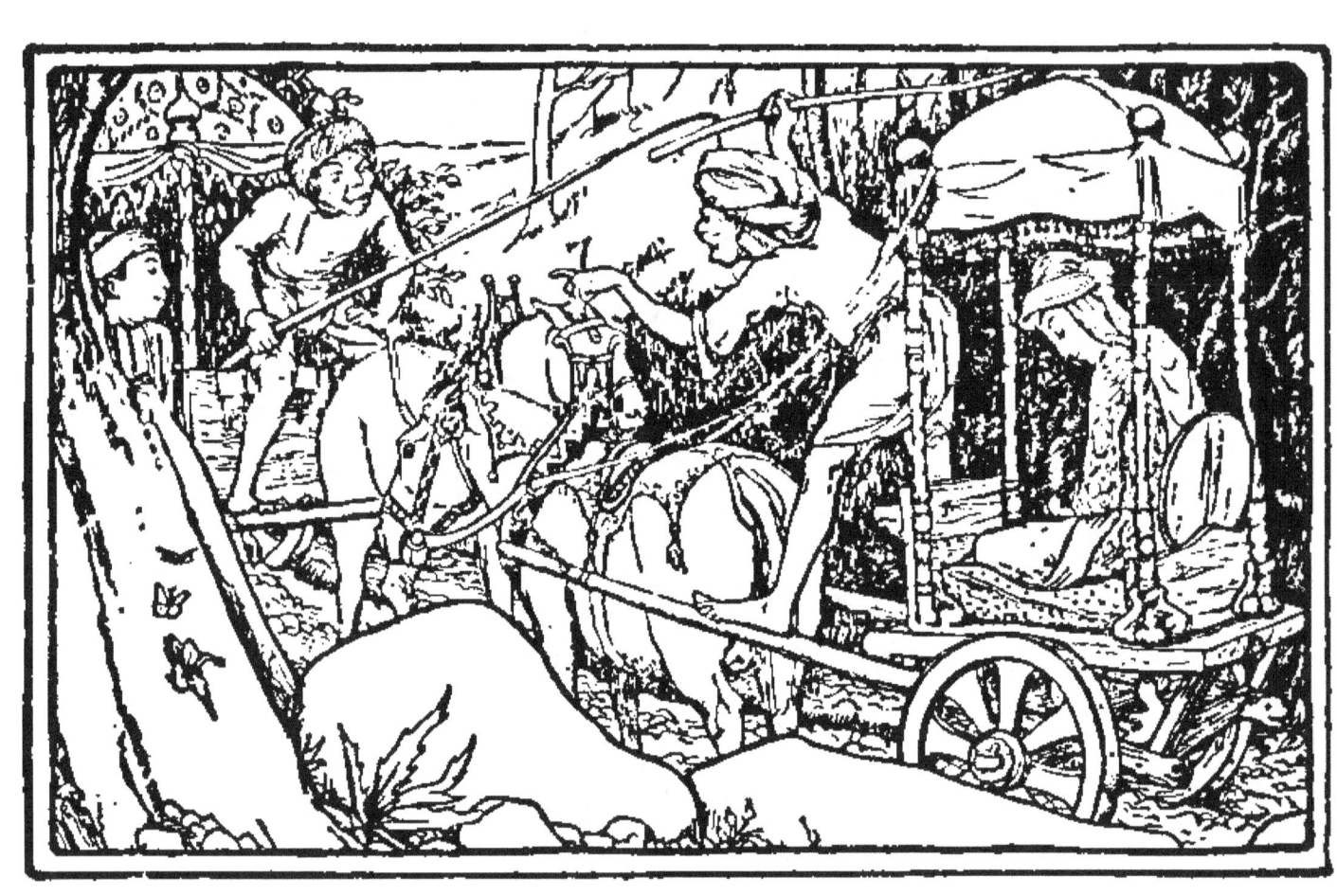

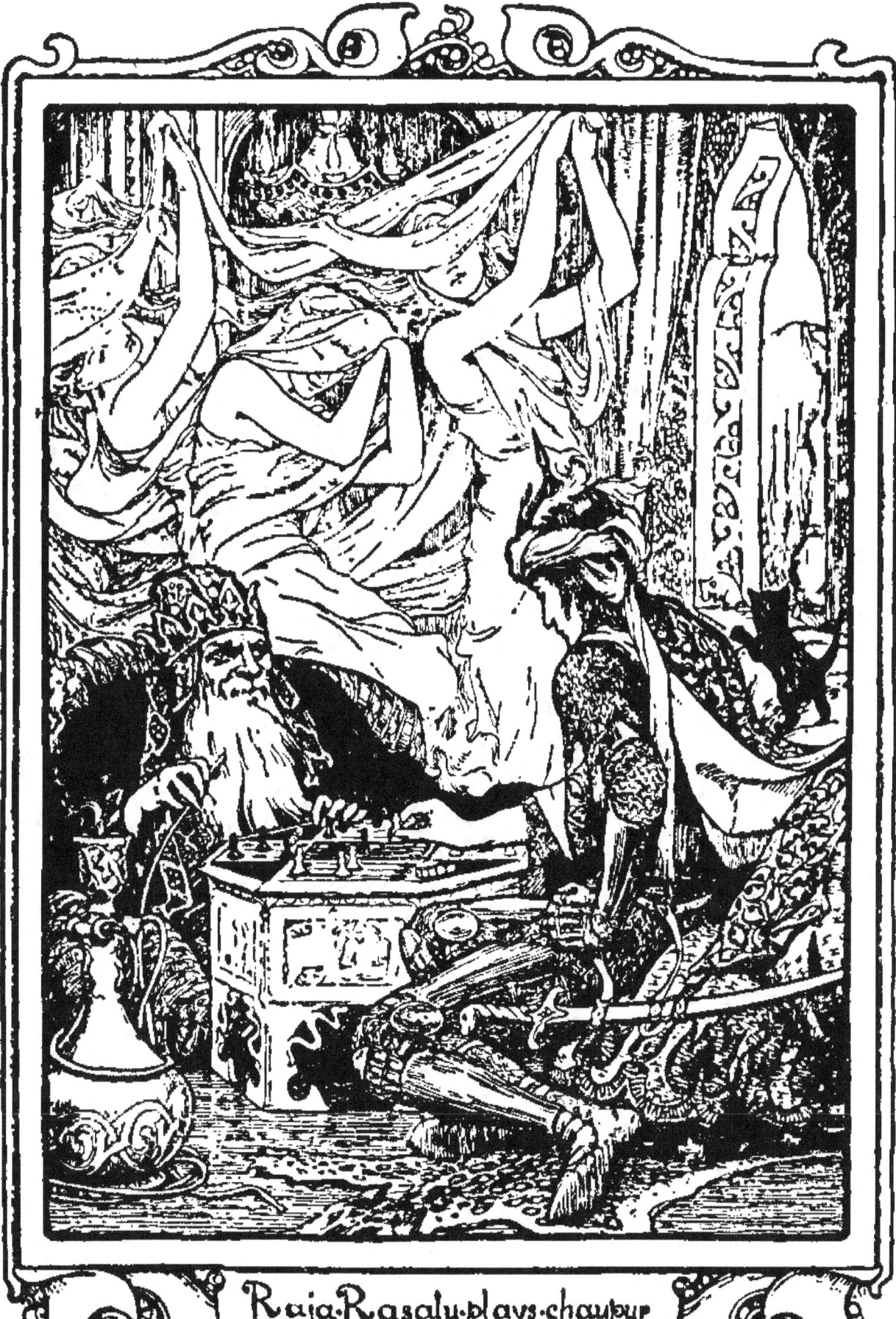
Raja Rasalu plays chaupur with Raja Sarkap.

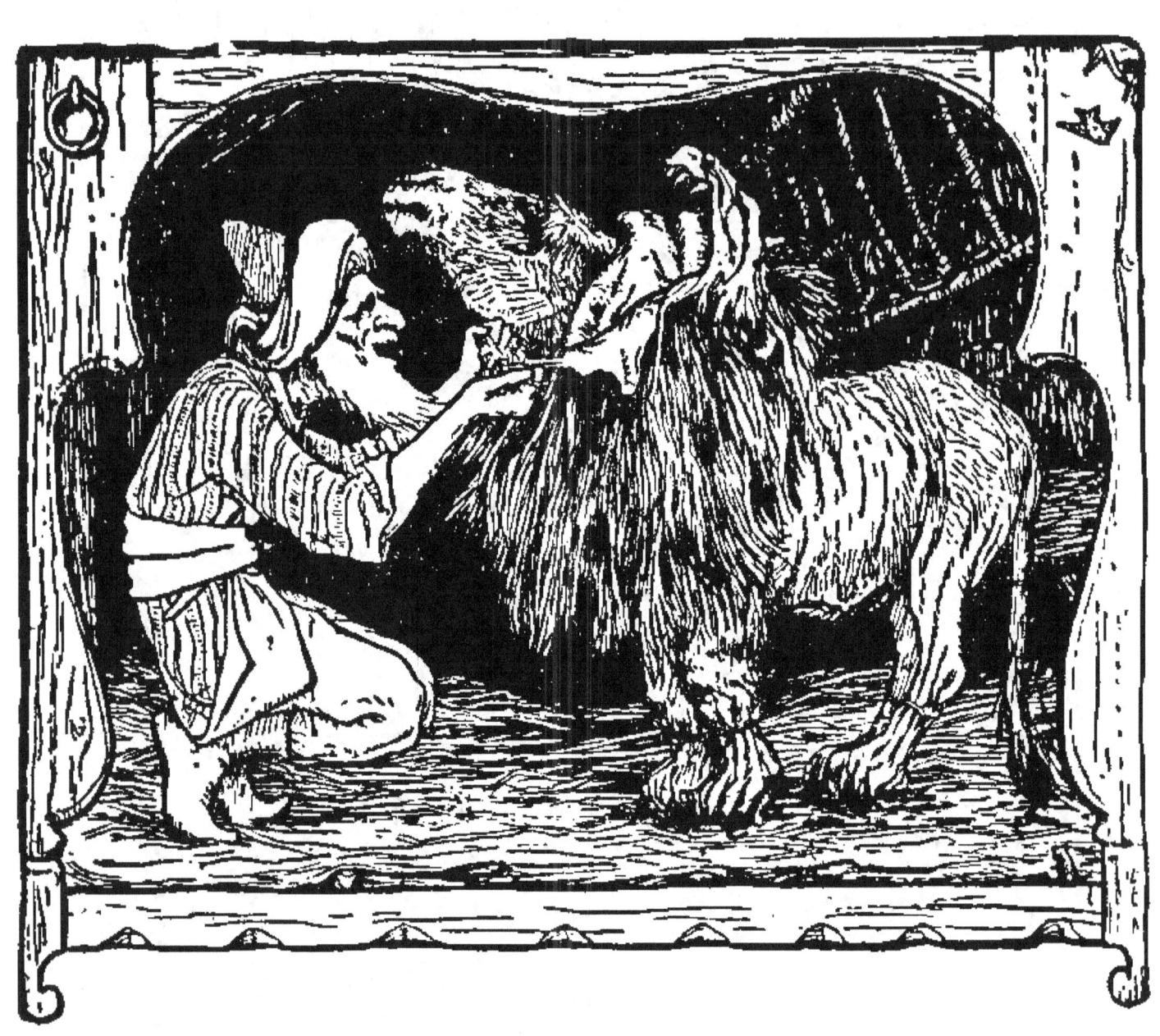

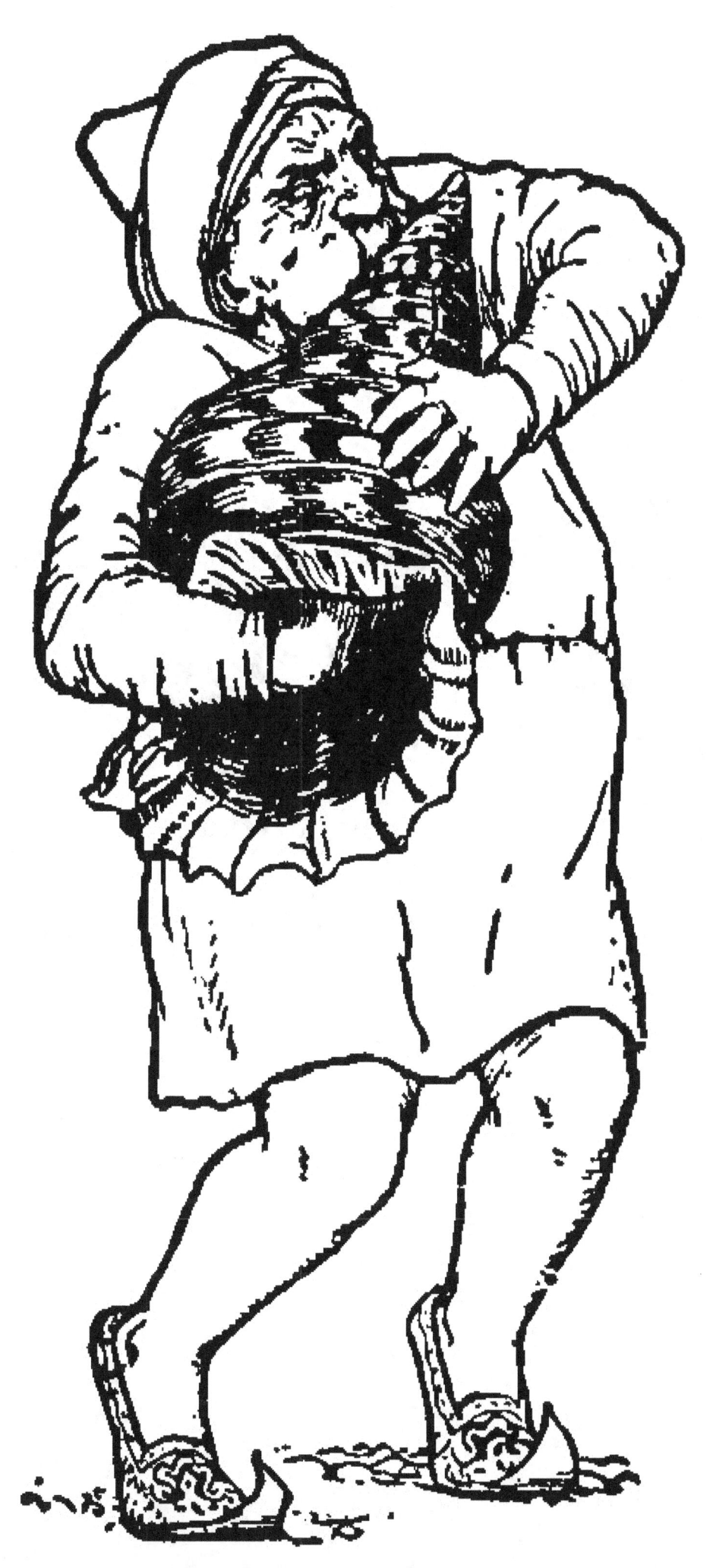

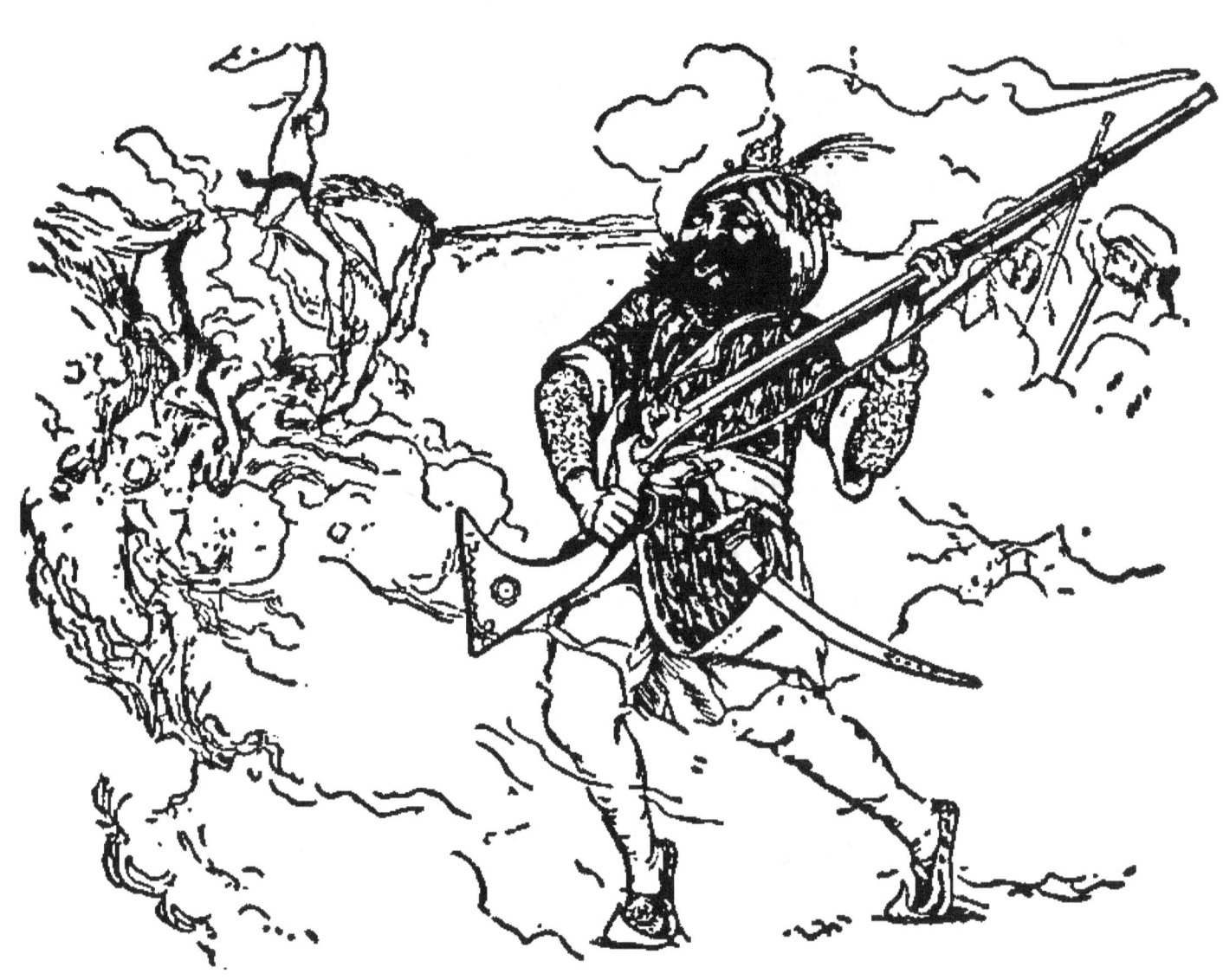

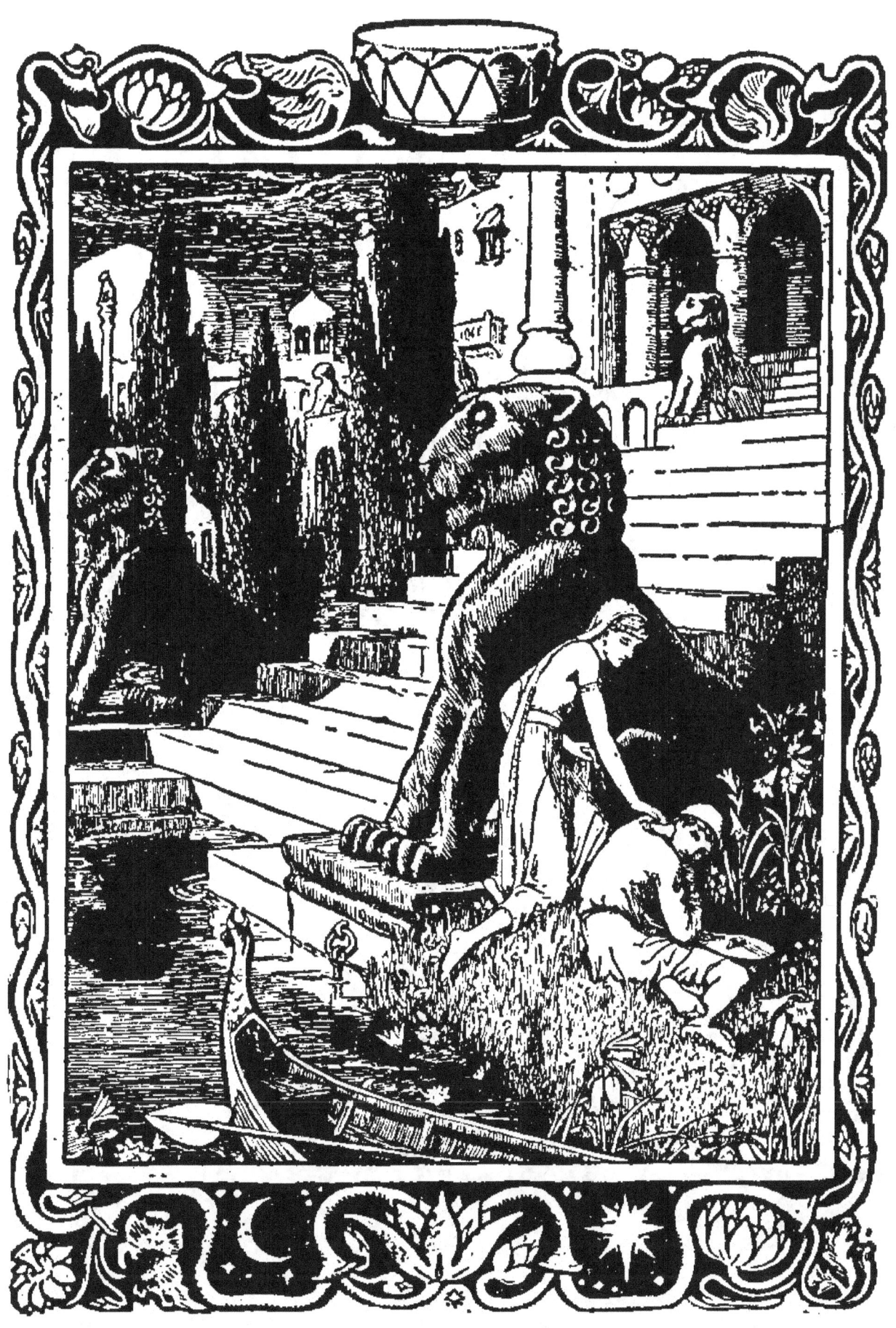

The Boy with the Moon on his Forehead

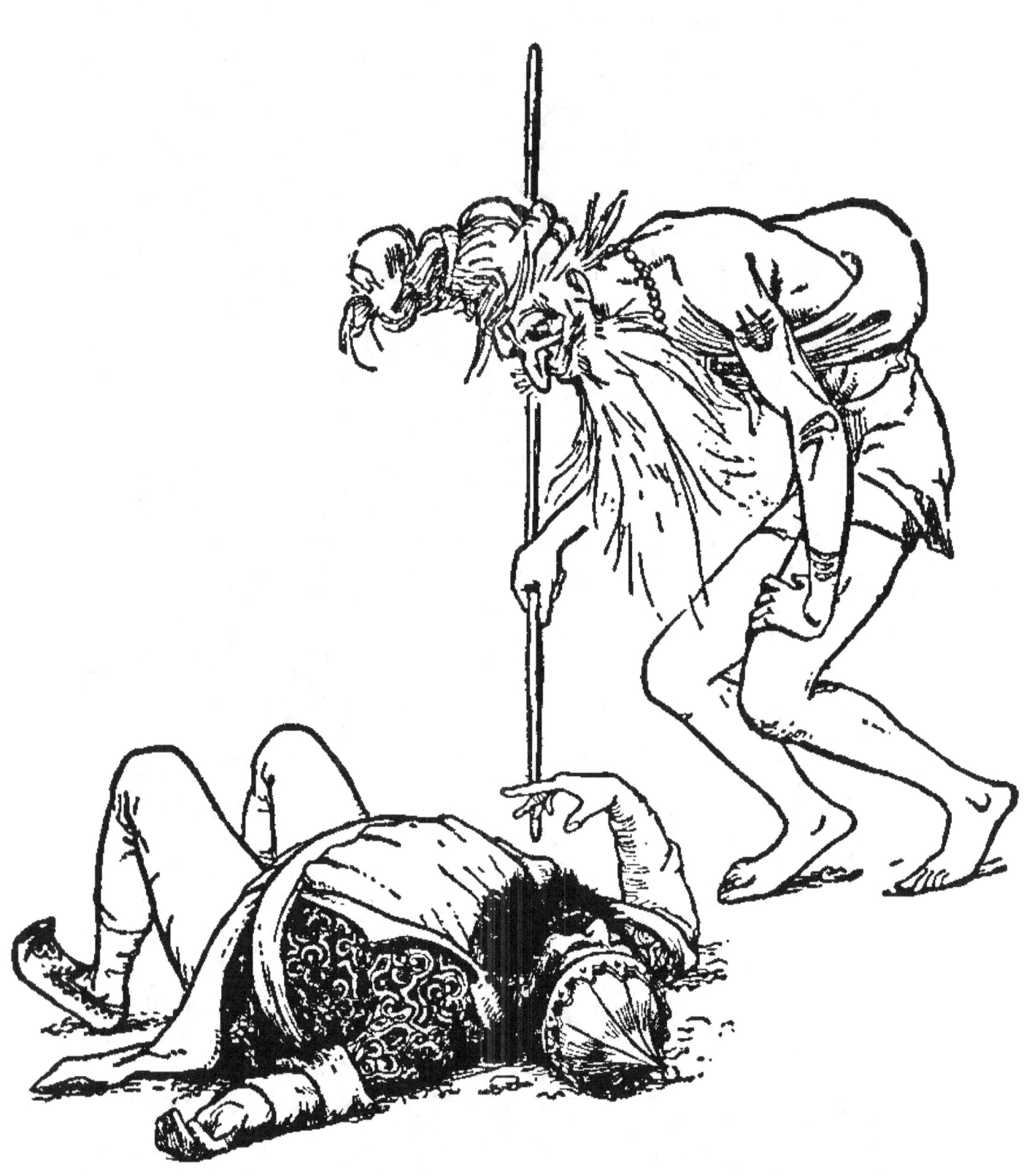

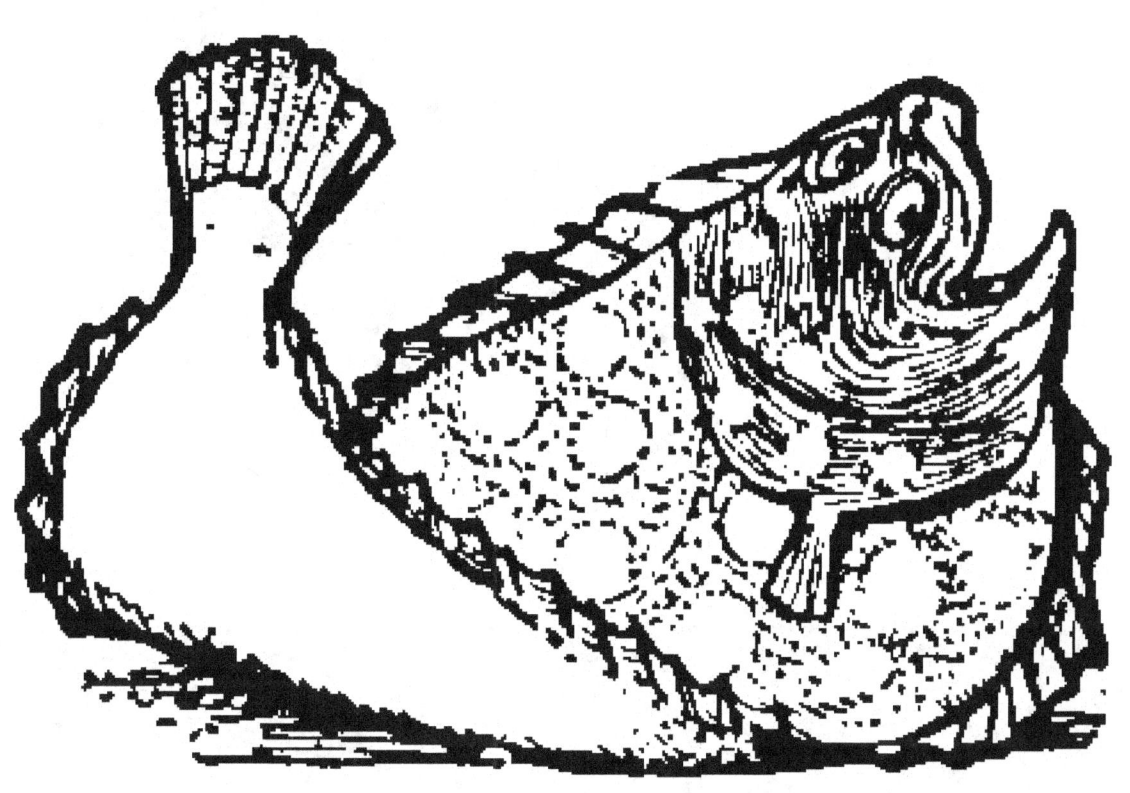

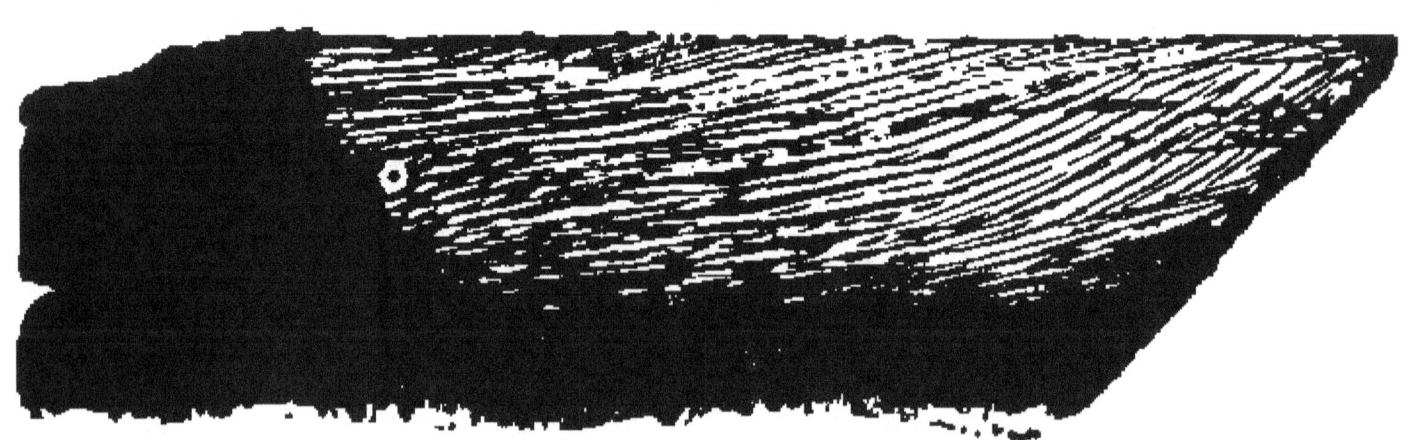

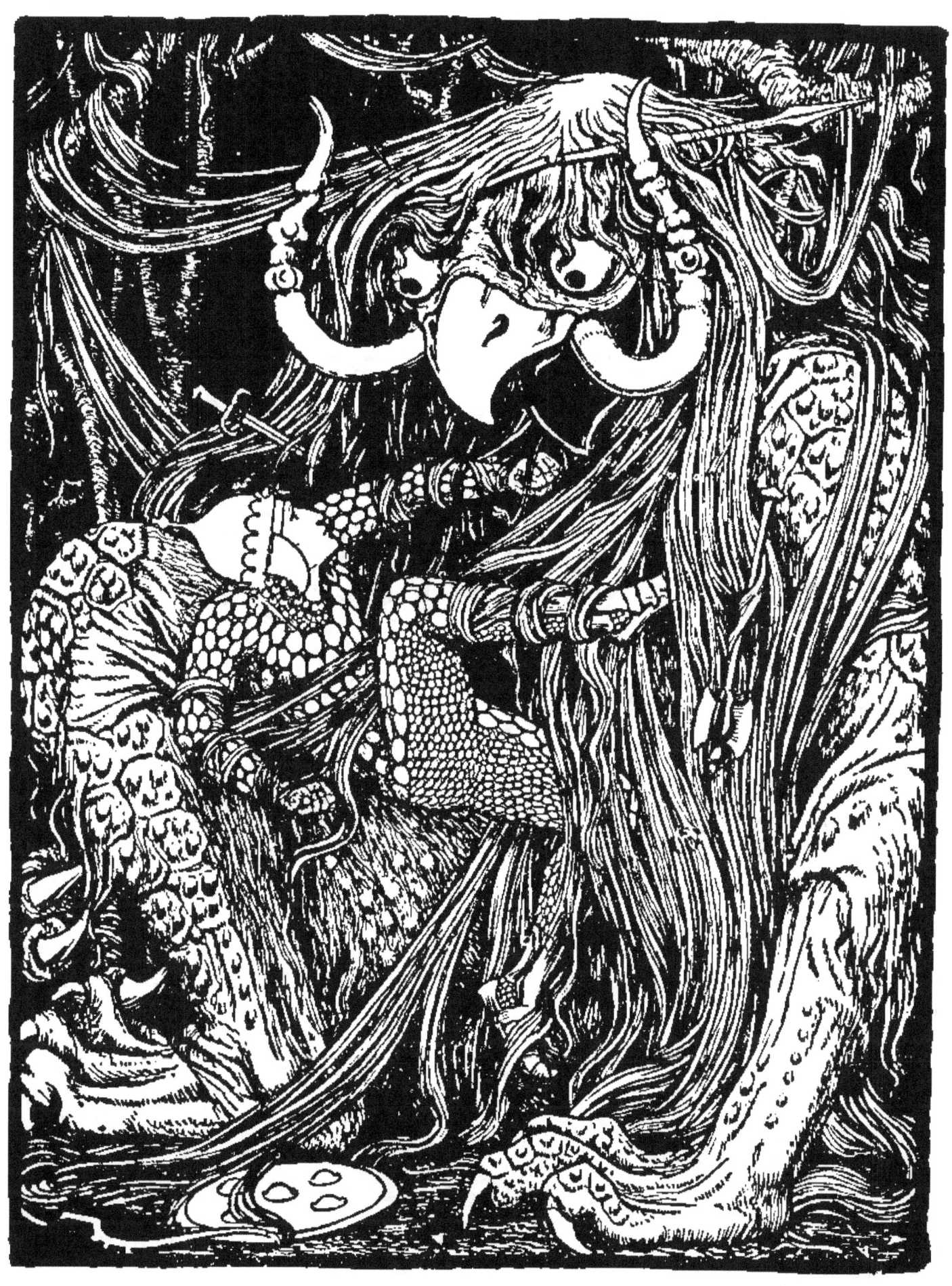

The Demon with the Matted Hair

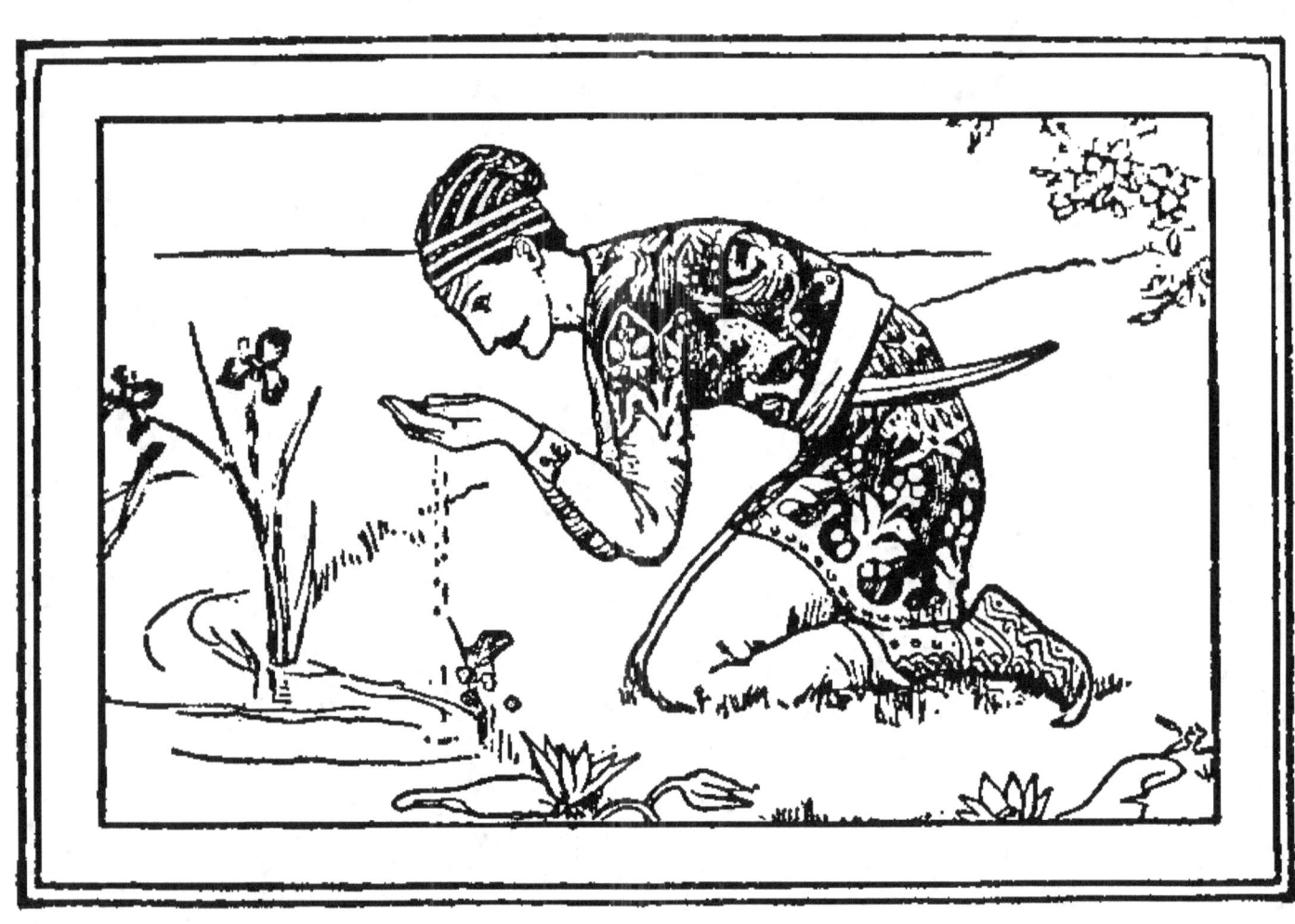

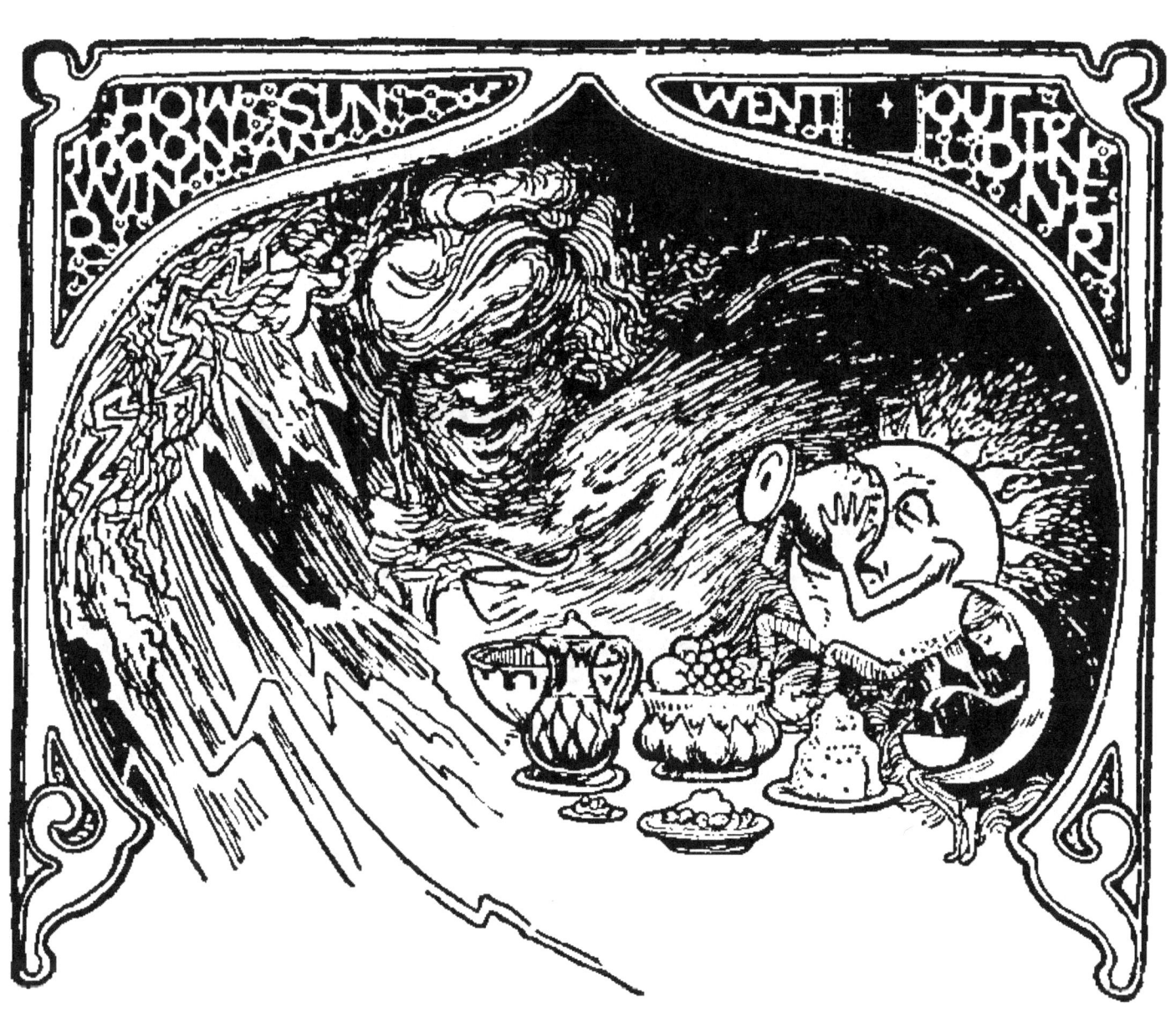

www.ingramcontent.com/pod-product-compliance
Lightning Source LLC
Chambersburg PA
CBHW082123220526
45472CB00009B/2283